RATIONAL EMOTIVE

IN

Action

KT-162-455

COUNSELLING
· IN ACTION ·

Series editor: Windy Dryden

Counselling in Action is a series of books developed
especially for counsellors and students of
counselling which provides clear and explicit
guidelines for counselling practice. A special feature
of the series is the emphasis it places on the *process*
of counselling.

Feminist Counselling in Action
Jocelyn Chaplin

Gestalt Counselling in Action
Petrūska Clarkson

Trancultural Counselling in Action
Patricia d'Ardenne and Aruna Mahtani

Key Issues for Counselling in Action
edited by Windy Dryden

Rational-Emotive Counselling in Action
Windy Dryden

Psychodynamic Counselling in Action
Michael Jacobs

Experiences of Counselling in Action
edited by Dave Mearns and Windy Dryden

Person-Centred Counselling in Action
Dave Mearns and Brian Thorne

Transactional Analysis Counselling in Action
Ian Stewart

Cognitive-Behavioural Counselling in Action
Peter Trower, Andrew Casey and Windy Dryden

RATIONAL-EMOTIVE
COUNSELLING

WINDY DRYDEN

SAGE Publications

London • Thousand Oaks • New Delhi

Preface, Parts 1–3 and Appendix 1 © Windy Dryden 1990

First published 1990
Reprinted 1992, 1993, 1994, 1996

Appendix 2, *How to Maintain and Enhance Your Rational-Emotive Therapy Gains* © Albert Ellis 1984, and reprinted by kind permission of Albert Ellis and the Institute for Rational-Emotive Therapy.

 SAGE Publications Ltd
6 Bonhill Street
London EC2A 4PU

SAGE Publications Inc
2455 Teller Road
Thousand Oaks, California 91320

SAGE Publications India Pvt Ltd
32, M-Block Market
Greater Kailash – I
New Delhi 110 048

British Library Cataloguing in Publication Data

Dryden, Windy
   Rational-emotive counselling in action.
   1. Medicine. Rational-emotive therapy
   I. Title   II. Series
   616.89′4

   ISBN 0-8039-8269-0
   ISBN 0-8039-8270-4 Pbk

Library of Congress catalog card number 89–062942

Typeset by Photoprint, Torquay, Devon
Printed in Great Britain by J.W. Arrowsmith, Bristol

Contents

Preface

My goal in this book has been to present the essence of rational-emotive counselling *in action*. To this end I have structured the book in three parts. In Part 1, I outline the basic theoretical and practical principles of rational-emotive counselling. In Part 2, I detail a sequence of thirteen steps that you need to follow when attempting to help your client with any given problem using rational-emotive counselling. Finally, in Part 3, I consider the process of rational-emotive counselling from beginning to end. To highlight rational-emotive counselling *in action* I have presented the case of Steve (a pseudonym) who you will meet in Parts 2 and 3 of the book.

Because I have restricted myself to presenting the essence of rational-emotive counselling, I have given scant attention to more general counselling issues which are adequately covered in other volumes in this series (see, in particular, Dryden, 1989; Stewart, 1989). I have also largely omitted references to other cognitive and cognitive-behavioural approaches to counselling which rational-emotive counsellors may draw upon, again because this material appears in another volume in this series (Trower et al., 1988).

I wish to thank Peter Hood, Richard House, Peva Keane, and Avril Love for their help in the preparation of this manuscript. Finally, I wish to compliment past and present staff members at Sage for their superb work on all volumes in this series. Thank you Alison, David, Farrell, Nicola, Sue, Susan, and Vivienne.

This book is dedicated to Ray DiGiuseppe, Jack Gordon, Paul Hauck, Al Raitt and Joe Yankura. Thank you for your help and support.

References

Dryden, W. (ed.) (1989) *Key Issues for Counselling in Action.* London: Sage.
Stewart, I. (1989) *Transactional Analysis Counselling in Action.* London: Sage.
Trower, P., Casey, A., and Dryden, W. (1988) *Cognitive-Behavioural Counselling in Action.* London: Sage.

Windy Dryden, London
May, 1989

PART 1 THE BASIC PRINCIPLES OF RATIONAL-EMOTIVE COUNSELLING

In this first part of the book I will first consider the theoretical underpinnings of rational-emotive counselling and then focus on the key practical elements of this counselling approach.

Theoretical Underpinnings of Rational-Emotive Counselling

Historical Context

Rational-emotive therapy (RET) was originated in 1955 by Albert Ellis, a New York clinical psychologist. Ellis originally worked as a psychoanalyst, and while he enjoyed practising this mode of therapy, he later became dissatisfied with it because it was, in his words, 'inefficient', in that it took a long time and did not produce very effective therapeutic results. For a while Ellis experimented with the shorter-term psychoanalytic psychotherapy and with various eclectic approaches before he founded RET. In doing so he was influenced more by philosophers than by psychologists, returning to a long-standing interest in practical approaches within the philosophic tradition. In particular he was influenced by the views of Epictetus, a Roman philosopher, who stated that 'men are disturbed not by things but by their views of things'.

At that time in the mid-1950s most therapists were influenced by psychoanalytic theories and methods and thus, to emphasise the logical and cognitive disputing aspects of his therapeutic approach, Ellis called his method 'rational therapy'. This caused problems in that it was generally assumed that rational therapy only involved a focus on cognition (that is, thoughts and beliefs). However, right from the start Ellis held that cognition, emotion, and behaviour were interrelated psychological processes and that his approach to therapy emphasised all three. In order to counter further unwarranted criticisms that were made about rational therapy, namely that it neglected emotion, Ellis retitled his approach to psychotherapy 'rational-emotive therapy' in 1961, a point which was stressed in the title of Ellis's first major book on RET, entitled *Reason and Emotion in Psychotherapy* (Ellis, 1962). While the name rational-emotive therapy has remained unchanged to this day, Ellis has argued that his approach could easily have been called rational-emotive-behaviour therapy in that, in addition to focusing on clients' emotions and beliefs, rational-emotive counsellors encourage their clients actively to put into practice what they learn in therapy through the use of behavioural methods.

Goals, Purposes, and Rationality

According to rational-emotive theory humans are happiest when they set up important life goals and purposes and actively strive to achieve these. In doing so, we had better acknowledge that we live in a social world and thus we are encouraged to develop a philosophy of enlightened self-interest. This involves pursuing our valued goals while demonstrating what Alfred Adler called social interest — a commitment to both helping others achieve their valued goals and to making the world a socially and environmentally better place in which to live.

Given that we tend to be goal-directed, *rational* in RET theory means 'that which helps people to achieve their basic goals and purposes, whereas irrational means that which prevents them from achieving these goals and purposes' (Dryden, 1984: 238). While rationality is not defined in any absolute sense, it does have three major criteria: namely, it is (a) pragmatic; (b) logical; and (c) reality-based. Thus, a more extended definition of rationality would be, first, that which helps people to achieve their basic goals and purposes; secondly, that which is logical (non-absolutist); and thirdly, that which is empirically consistent with reality. Conversely, an extended definition of irrationality would be, first, that which prevents people from achieving their basic goals and purposes; secondly, that which is illogical (especially, dogmatic and musturbatory); and thirdly, that which is empirically inconsistent with reality.

Responsible Hedonism

Rational-emotive theory argues that as humans we are basically hedonistic in the sense that we seek to stay alive and to achieve a reasonable degree of happiness. Here hedonism does not mean 'the pleasures of the flesh' but involves the concept of personal meaning; a person can be said to be acting hedonistically when she is happy acting in a way that is personally meaningful for her. The concept of responsible hedonism means once again that we are mindful of the fact that we live in a social world and that ideally our personally meaningful actions should help to make the world a better place in which to live, or at the very least should not unduly harm anyone.

Rational-emotive theory makes an important distinction between short- and long-range hedonism. We are likely to be at our happiest when we succeed in achieving both our short-term and our long-term goals. Frequently, however, we defeat ourselves by attempting to satisfy our short-term goals while at the same time sabotaging our long-term goals. Thus, for example we often strive to avoid discomfort when it would be advisable for us to experience discomfort because doing so would help us to achieve our long-term goals. Rational-emotive counsellors encourage their clients to achieve a balance between the pursuit of their short- and long-range goals, while being mindful of the fact that what represents a healthy balance for a given person is best judged by that person.

Enlightened Self-interest
Rational-emotive counsellors have often been accused of advocating selfishness since they do encourage their clients in the pursuit of happiness. However, this is not so if we define selfishness as 'the ruthless pursuit of one's goals while cynically disregarding the goals and viewpoints of others'. Rather, rational-emotive counsellors encourage their clients to demonstrate enlightened self-interest, which involves putting themselves first most of the time while putting others, and particularly significant others, a close second. Enlightened self-interest also sometimes involves putting the desires of others before our own, particularly when the welfare and happiness of these others are of great importance to them and our desires are not primary. Self-sacrifice is discouraged unless the person wants to sacrifice herself and finds personal meaning and happiness in doing so.

Philosophic and Scientific Emphasis
Rational-emotive theory stresses that we are born philosophers. We have the ability to think about our thinking and to realise that we are highly influenced by our implicit philosophies of life which are either flexible and undogmatic or musturbatory and absolutist. Rational-emotive theory agrees with the ideas of George Kelly (1955) that we are also scientists and are able to appreciate that our philosophies are basically hypotheses about ourselves, other people, and the world which need to be tested. This is best done together with our philosophical abilities, particularly our ability to think critically about the logical and illogical aspects of our thought.

While Ellis (1976) has argued that humans have a strong tendency to think and act irrationally, we also have the ability to think critically about our thinking and behaviour and to correct the illogicalities in our thinking as well as to judge whether or not our hypotheses are consistent with reality. Rational-emotive theorists do, however, appreciate that reality cannot be judged in any absolute manner but is best regarded as accurate if it is seen as such by a group of neutral observers (the principle of consensual reality).

Humanistic Outlook

RET is not only philosophical and scientific in orientation but it takes a specific humanistic-existential approach to human problems and their solutions. This view conceptualises humans as holistic, indivisible, goal-directed organisms who have importance in the world just because we are human and alive. It encourages us to accept ourselves unconditionally with our limitations while at the same time encouraging us to work towards minimising our limitations. RET agrees with the position of ethical humanism which 'encourages people to live by rules emphasising human interests over the interests of inanimate nature, of lower animals or of any assumed natural order or deity' (Ellis, 1980: 327). However, this does not mean being ecologically or environmentally insensitive, advocating the mindless slaughter of animals or being disrespectful of others' religious views. Furthermore, this outlook acknowledges that we are human and are in no way superhuman or subhuman.

Two Basic Biologically Based Tendencies

Rational-emotive theory hypothesises that as humans we have a biologically based tendency to think irrationally as well as a similar tendency to think rationally. It thus differs from other approaches to counselling in emphasising the power of these biologically based tendencies over the power of environmental conditions to affect human happiness, although it by no means neglects the contribution of these environmental conditions to influence human emotion and behaviour. The view that irrational thinking is largely determined by biological factors, albeit always interacting with influential environmental conditions, rests on the seeming ease with which humans think crookedly and the prevalence of such thinking even among those humans who have been rationally raised. Ellis has noted in this regard that 'even if everybody had had the most rational upbringing, virtually all humans would often irrationally escalate their individual and social preferences into absolutistic demands on (a) themselves (b) other people and (c) the universe around them' (Ellis, 1984a: 20).[1]

Two Fundamental Human Disturbances

Ellis has noted that human psychological problems can be loosely divided into two major categories: ego disturbance and discomfort disturbance. Ego disturbance relates to the demands that we make about ourselves and the consequent negative self-ratings that we make when we fail to live up to our self-imposed demands. Furthermore, ego-disturbance issues may underpin what at first glance appear to be demands made of others or of life conditions. Thus, I may be angry at you because you are acting in a way which I perceive as a threat to my 'self-esteem'. The fact that my anger is directed outwardly towards you serves in this way to protect my own 'shaky self-esteem'.

Discomfort disturbance, on the other hand, is more related to the domain of human comfort and occurs when we make dogmatic commands that comfort and comfortable life conditions must exist.

As will be shown later in this part of the book, the healthy alternative to ego disturbance rests on a fundamental attitude of unconditional self-acceptance where a person fully accepts herself as being a human and unable to be given a single global rating. The healthy alternative to discomfort disturbance rests on a philosophy of a high frustration or discomfort tolerance where we are prepared to tolerate frustration or discomfort, not for its own sake, but as a way of overcoming obstacles to the pursuit of our basic goals and purposes.

Psychological Interactionism

Rational-emotive theory states that a person's thoughts, emotions and actions cannot be treated separately from one another. Rather, they are best conceptualised as being overlapping or interacting psychological processes. This is the principle of psychological interactionism. Thus, when I think about something I have a tendency to have an emotional reaction towards it and also a tendency to act towards it in some way. Also, if I have a feeling about a person then I am likely to have some thought about him and also, again, a tendency to act towards him in a certain manner. Similarly, if I act in a certain manner this is often based on my thoughts and feelings towards either an object or a person.

RET is perhaps best known for the emphasis that it places on cognition and for its cognitive restructuring components. While it is true that it does emphasise the power of cognition in human happiness and disturbance, it does so while fully acknowledging the affective and behavioural components of human functioning. It stresses that these three fundamental human psychological processes almost always interact and often in complex ways (Ellis, 1985a). Similarly, while the practice of rational-emotive counselling is perhaps known for its cognitive restructuring methods, these are by no means the sole ingredients of the approach and rational-emotive counsellors frequently use emotive-evocative and behavioural methods to encourage clients to change their thinking.

The ABC Framework

The ABC framework is the cornerstone of RET practice and therefore it merits detailed attention. A stands for an activating event which may be external or internal to your client. When A refers to an external event we can say that it actually occurred if your client's descriptions of it can be confirmed as accurate by neutral observers (the principle of consensual reality). In this book, however, A will also stand for your client's inference (or interpretation) about the event.[2]

B stands for beliefs. These are evaluative cognitions or constructed views of the world which are either rigid or flexible. When these beliefs are rigid they are called *irrational beliefs* and take the form of musts, absolute shoulds, have to's, got to's and so on. When your clients adhere to such rigid beliefs they will also tend to make irrational conclusions from these irrational premises. These irrational conclusions take the form of: (a) *awfulising* — meaning more than 100 per cent bad, worse than it absolutely should be; (b) *I-can't-stand-it-itis* (or low frustration tolerance) — meaning that your clients cannot envisage enduring situations or having any happiness at all if what they demand must not exist actually exists; (c) *damnation* — here your clients will damn themselves, other people, and/or life conditions; and (d) *always and never thinking* — your clients will insist, for example, that they will always fail or never will be approved by significant others.

When your client's beliefs are flexible they are called *rational beliefs* in RET. Flexible beliefs often take the form of desires, wishes, wants, and preferences, which your clients do *not* escalate into dogmatic musts, shoulds, oughts, and so on. When your clients adhere to such flexible rational beliefs they will tend to make rational conclusions from these rational premises. These conclusions take the form of (a) *evaluations of badness* — here, for example, your clients will conclude 'it's bad, but not terrible' rather than 'it's awful' when faced with a negative activating event; (b) *statements of toleration* — here your clients may say 'I don't like it, but I can bear it'; (c) *acceptance of fallibility* — here your clients will accept themselves and other people as fallible human beings who cannot legitimately be given a single global rating. Also your clients will accept the world and life conditions as complex, composed of good, bad, and neutral elements, and thus will also refrain from giving the world a global rating; and (d) *flexible thinking with respect to the occurrence of events* — here your clients will refrain from thinking that something will always occur or will never happen. Rather, they realise that most events in the universe can be placed along a continuum from 'occurring very rarely' to 'occurring very frequently'.

C in the ABC framework stands for emotional and behavioural consequences of your client's beliefs about A. In RET, the C's that follow from irrational rigid beliefs about negative A's will be disturbed and are called *inappropriate* negative consequences and C's that follow from rational flexible beliefs about negative A's will be non-disturbed and are termed *appropriate* negative consequences (Crawford and Ellis, 1989). Inappropriate negative emotions are inappropriate for any one or more of the following reasons: they lead to the experience of a great deal of psychic pain and discomfort; they motivate one to engage in self-defeating behaviour; and they prevent one from carrying out behaviour necessary to reach one's goals. Conversely, appropriate negative emotions are appropriate for any one or more of the following reasons: they alert one that one's goals are being blocked but do not immobilise one; they motivate one to engage in self-enhancing behaviour; and they encourage the successful execution of behaviour necessary to reach one's goals.

Three Basic Musts
While your clients will often express their irrational beliefs in personally distinctive terms, you might find it helpful to consider these individualistic beliefs to be variations of three 'basic musts'.

Basic Must No. 1: Demands about Self   The first basic must concerns your clients' demands about themselves and is often stated in these terms: '*I* must do well and be approved by significant others and if I'm not, then it is awful; I can't stand it, and I am a damnable person to some degree when I am not loved or when I do not do well.' These beliefs often lead to anxiety, depression, shame, and guilt.

Basic Must No. 2: Demands about Others   The second basic must concerns your clients' demands about other people, and is often expressed as follows: '*You* must treat me well and justly, and it's awful and I can't bear it when you don't. *You* are damnable when you don't treat me well and you deserve to be punished for doing what you must not do.' Such beliefs are often associated with feelings of anger, rage, passive-aggressiveness, and acts of violence.

Basic Must No. 3: Demands about the World/Life Conditions   The third basic must concerns your clients' demands about the world or *life conditions* and often takes the following form: 'Life conditions under which I live absolutely must be the way I want them to be and if they are not, it's terrible, I can't stand it, poor me.' This belief is associated with feelings of self-pity and hurt, and problems of self-discipline — for example, procrastination and addictive behaviour.

The Disturbance Matrix

It is possible to take the three basic musts and the two fundamental human disturbances to form a 3 × 2 disturbance matrix (see Figure 1).

	Ego disturbance	Discomfort disturbance
I must	A	B
You must	C	D
Life conditions must	E	F

Figure 1 *The disturbance matrix*

(A) *Ego Disturbance — Demands about Self*   In this type of disturbance it is quite clear that the person concerned is making demands about himself and the issue concerns his attitude towards himself. Thus, the major derivative from the demand concerns some variation of self-damnation: for example, 'I must obtain a good degree and if I don't I am no good.'

(B) *Discomfort Disturbance — Demands about Self*   Here the person makes demands about himself but the real issue concerns his attitude towards discomfort: for example, 'I must obtain a good degree because if I don't, life conditions will be terrible.'

(C) *Ego Disturbance — Demands about Others*   Here the person makes demands about another person, but the real issue concerns his attitude towards himself. A common example of this is found when another person's behaviour serves as a threat to the person's self-esteem and his anger about the other's behaviour serves to protect his self-esteem: for example, 'You must treat me nicely because if you do not then that proves that I am no good.'

(D) *Discomfort Disturbance — Demands about Others* Here the person makes demands about others but the real issue concerns the realm of discomfort: for example, 'You must treat me nicely because I couldn't stand life conditions if you do not.'

(E) *Ego Disturbance — Demands about Life Conditions* Here, on the surface, the person makes demands about some aspect of life conditions, but the real issue concerns his attitude towards himself: for example, 'Life conditions must be easy for me because if they are not then that's just proof of my worthlessness.'

(F) *Discomfort Disturbance — Demands about Life Conditions* This kind of disturbance is a more impersonal form of low frustration tolerance. It is often seen when a person loses his temper with inanimate objects: for example, 'My car absolutely must not break down because I couldn't stand the frustration if it did.'

Distinction between Appropriate and Inappropriate Negative Emotions

I earlier made a distinction between appropriate and inappropriate negative emotions (see p. 7). In this context it is important to realise that people can hold rational and irrational beliefs at the same time, and they can easily escalate their desires into demands. Thus, I may rationally believe that 'I want to get a good degree' and simultaneously believe that, 'Since I want to get a good degree, I must achieve one.' Consequently, it is important for counsellors to discriminate between their clients' rational and irrational beliefs. When such distinctions are made it is easier to distinguish between appropriate and inappropriate negative emotions. To reiterate the point made on p. 7 appropriate negative emotions are associated with rational beliefs and inappropriate negative emotions with irrational beliefs.

I will now consider the distinction between appropriate and inappropriate negative emotions in greater detail. In the emotions that follow the appropriate negative emotion is listed first.

Concern vs. Anxiety Concern is an emotion that is associated with the belief, 'I hope that this threat does not happen, but if it does, it would be unfortunate', whereas anxiety occurs when the person believes, 'This threat must not happen and it would be awful if it did.'

Sadness vs. Depression   Sadness is deemed to occur when the person believes, 'It is very unfortunate that I have experienced this loss but there is no reason why it should not have happened.' Depression, on the other hand, is associated with the belief, 'This loss should not have occurred and it is terrible that it did.' Here, when the person feels responsible for the loss, he or she will tend to damn him or herself: '*I* am no good', whereas if the loss is outside the person's control he or she will tend to damn the world/life conditions: '*It* is terrible.' RET theory holds that it is the philosophy of musturbation implicit in such evaluations that leads the person to consider that he or she will never get what he or she wants, an inference that leads to feelings of hopelessness. Thus, for example: 'Because I must always get the things I really want and did not get it this time, I'll never get it at all. It's hopeless!'

Regret vs. Guilt   Feelings of regret or remorse occur when a person acknowledges that he has done something bad in public or private but accepts himself as a fallible human being for doing so. The person feels badly about the act or deed but not about himself because he holds the belief, 'I prefer not to act badly, but if I do, too bad!' Guilt occurs when the person damns himself as bad, wicked, or rotten for acting badly. Here, the person feels badly both about the act and his 'self' because he holds the belief: 'I must not act badly and if I do it's *awful* and I am a *rotten* person!'

Disappointment vs. Shame/Embarrassment   Feelings of disappointment occur when a person acts 'stupidly' in public, acknowledges the stupid act, but accepts herself in the process. The person feels disappointed about her action but not with herself because she prefers but does not demand that she act well. Shame and embarrassment occur when the person again recognises that she has acted 'stupidly' in public and then condemns herself for acting in a way that she should not have done. People who experience shame and embarrassment often predict that the watching audience will think badly of them, in which case they tend to agree with these perceived judgements. Thus, they often believe that they absolutely need the approval of these others. Shame can sometimes be distinguished from embarrassment in that the public 'pratfall' is regarded by the person as more serious in shame. However, both emotions involve self-denigration.

Table 1   *Inappropriate and appropriate negative emotions and their cognitive correlates*

Inference[1] related to personal domain[2]	Type of belief	Emotion	Appropriate-ness of emotion
Threat or danger	Irrational	Anxiety	Inappropriate
Threat or danger	Rational	Concern	Appropriate
Loss (with implications for future); failure	Irrational	Depression	Inappropriate
Loss (with implications for future); failure	Rational	Sadness	Appropriate
Breaking of personal rule (other or self); other threatens self; frustration	Irrational	Damning anger	Inappropriate
Breaking of personal rule (other or self); other threatens self; frustration	Rational	Non-damning anger (or annoyance	Appropriate
Breaking of own moral code	Irrational	Guilt	Inappropriate
Breaking of own moral code	Rational	Remorse	Appropriate
Other betrays self (self non-deserving)	Irrational	Hurt	Inappropriate
Other betrays self (self non-deserving)	Rational	Disappointment	Appropriate
Threat to desired exclusive relationship	Irrational	Morbid jealousy	Inappropriate
Threat to desired exclusive relationship	Rational	Non-morbid jealousy	Appropriate
Personal weakness revealed publicly	Irrational	Shame/ Embarrassment	Inappropriate
Personal weakness revealed publicly	Rational	Regret	Appropriate

[1] Inference = An interpretation which goes beyond observable reality but which gives meaning to it; may be accurate or inaccurate.
[2] The objects — tangible and intangible — in which a person has an involvement constitute a person's personal domain (Beck, 1976). Rational-emotive theory distinguishes between ego and comfort aspects of the personal domain although these aspects frequently interact.

Annoyance vs. Anger   Annoyance occurs when another person disregards an individual's rule of living. The annoyed person does not like what the other has done but does not damn him or her for doing it. Such a person tends to believe, 'I wish the other person did not do that and I don't like what he/she did, but it does not follow that he/she must not break my rule.' In anger, however, the person does believe that the other absolutely must not break the rule and thus damns the other for doing so.

Table 1 gives an extended list of the major emotional problems for which clients seek counselling and their constructive alternatives. It presents both the type of belief and the inferences most commonly associated with each of the emotions listed in the table.

Acquisition and Perpetuation of Psychological Disturbance

Rational-emotive theory does not put forward an elaborate account of the way in which we as humans acquire psychological disturbance. This is because of the view discussed earlier that we have a biological tendency to think irrationally. However, rational-emotive theory does acknowledge that environmental variables do contribute to our tendency to make ourselves disturbed by our irrational beliefs. Thus, if I have been treated harshly by my parents I am more likely to make demands about myself and about uncomfortable life conditions than I would be if my parents had treated me well. However, this is not always the case and I have met people who have had a harsh upbringing but have made less demands on themselves, others, and life conditions than do some of my clients who have had a much more favourable upbringing. Thus, rational-emotive theory stresses that humans vary in their disturbability. The rational-emotive view of the acquisition of psychological disturbance can be encapsulated in the view that we as humans are not made disturbed simply by our experiences; rather we bring our ability to disturb ourselves to these experiences.

Rational-emotive theory does, however, put forward a more elaborate account of how we perpetuate our psychological disturbance. First, it argues that we do so because we lack three major insights: (a) psychological disturbance is primarily determined by musturbatory irrational beliefs that we hold about ourselves, others, and the world; (b) we remain disturbed by reindoctrinating ourselves in the present with these irrational beliefs; and (c) the only long-term way of overcoming psychological disturbance is to work against our irrational beliefs and against our tendency to think and act irrationally.

Secondly, RET theory contends that we perpetuate our psychological problems because we adhere to a philosophy of low frustration tolerance (LFT). Thus, we tend to be short-range hedonists and to believe that we cannot stand discomfort. Even when we realise that we disturb ourselves with our beliefs in the present, we tend to think that this awareness alone will lead us to overcome our problems. Clients who have LFT beliefs will do poorly in rational-emotive counselling and other forms of counselling as well because they steadfastly refuse to make themselves uncomfortable in the present so that they can become comfortable later. In particular they tend to procrastinate concerning putting into practice outside counselling sessions what they have learnt inside counselling sessions and will frequently make a variety of 'good excuses' as to why they failed to do their homework assignments.

A third major way in which we perpetuate our psychological disturbances is explained by the fact that we often make ourselves disturbed (secondary disturbances) about our original disturbances. Thus, clients often make themselves anxious about their anxiety, guilty about their anger, depressed about their depression, ashamed about their embarrassment, and so on. Unless clients tackle their secondary problems before their primary problems, they will quite often impede themselves from overcoming these primary disturbances. Thus, if a person condemns himself for his anger problem, he will get caught up in his self-blaming depression which will, in itself, tend to stop him from dealing with his primary anger problem.

Fourthly, rational-emotive counsellors agree with their psychoanalytic colleagues that we frequently employ defences to ward off threats to our ego and to our level of comfort. Using such defensive manoeuvres means that we can refrain from taking personal responsibility for our problems when they exist, preferring to blame others or life conditions for our problems. When this happens in counselling, such clients tend to resist the basic message of the rational-emotive approach, namely that they *make themselves* disturbed, because if they were to accept this responsibility then they would, for example, severely condemn themselves. Unless the ideas that underlie their defensiveness are uncovered and dealt with, then little progress is possible.

Fifthly, we often perpetuate our problems because we get some kind of payoff from having these problems. Thus, we may get a lot of attention from others for having psychological problems which we are loathe to do without, or our problems may protect us in our minds from having more severe problems. When a person receives some kind of payoff from having a psychological problem, such as attention from others, she is reluctant to work to overcome her problem because she may fear that she might lose the attention from others which she demands. When the psychological problem protects the person in her own mind from a more severe psychological problem then she will not be motivated to give up the existing emotional problem unless she can also be helped to deal with the problem that she fears she might encounter.

Finally, we often perpetuate our own problems because we make self-fulfilling prophecies. Thus, a man who has difficulties in trusting women may, when he meets a new woman, be quite suspicious of her and indirectly discourage her from having warm intimate feelings towards him. This may lead to her leaving him which would confirm in his mind his original idea that women were not to be trusted. Unless clients who make self-fulfilling prophecies are encouraged to see the contribution that they make to these prophecies, they are likely to persist in perpetuating their problems.

Theory of Therapeutic Change
The rational-emotive theory of therapeutic change is basically a simple one. It states that if clients are to overcome their emotional and behavioural problems, they need to: (a) acknowledge that they have a problem; (b) identify and overcome any secondary disturbances about this problem; (c) identify the irrational belief that underpins the primary problem; (d) understand why their irrational belief is, in fact, irrational (that is, illogical, inconsistent with reality, and will give them poor results in life); (e) realise why the rational alternative to this irrational belief is logical, consistent with reality, and will give them better results; (f) challenge their irrational belief so that they begin to strengthen their conviction in the rational alternative; (g) use a variety of cognitive, emotive, imaginal and behavioural assignments to strengthen their conviction in their rational belief and weaken their conviction in their irrational belief; (h) identify and overcome obstacles to therapeutic change using the same sequence as above while accepting themselves for their tendency to construct such obstacles; and (i) keep working against their tendency to think and act irrationally.

Key Elements in Rational-Emotive Practice

The Goals of Rational-Emotive Counselling
Rational-emotive counselling is a system of counselling which is designed to help people to minimise their emotional disturbances and self-defeating behaviour and to encourage them to live a more meaningful and happier existence. In doing so, rational-emotive

counsellors help their clients to consider ways in which they prevent themselves from actualising themselves by focusing on the irrational beliefs that underpin their emotional and behavioural problems. Rational-emotive counsellors, then, encourage their clients: (a) to think more rationally (logically, flexibly, and scientifically); (b) to feel more appropriately; and (c) to act more efficiently in order to achieve their basic goals and purposes.

A standard goal is to encourage clients to identify their primary and secondary emotional and behavioural problems and to overcome these. However, a more ideal goal — and one that not all clients attain — is to encourage clients to make a profound philosophic change — meaning that they will: (a) give up making demands on themselves, others, and the world; (b) refrain from making dogmatic exaggerated ratings of themselves, others, and the world; (c) accept themselves and other people as fallible human beings; and (d) accept the world as being too complex to merit a global rating. Thus, rational-emotive counsellors encourage their clients to get over the emotional and behavioural problems for which they seek counselling in the first place and wherever possible encourage them to minimise their tendency to disturb and to defeat themselves.

While rational-emotive counsellors pursue this ideal goal of encouraging clients to make a profound philosophic change whenever possible, they acknowledge that their clients may not be interested in making such a radical shift in their personalities and they also recognise that many clients may not be able to embark on such a radical project. Thus, while rational-emotive counsellors offer their clients an opportunity to embark on a more radical restructuring of their personalities, they are flexible in adjusting their goals to meet their clients' goals.[3]

This flexibility is also shown in the work of rational-emotive counsellors with clients who are either unable or unwilling to work towards developing a new rational philosophy about specific elements of their lives. In such cases, rational-emotive counsellors will modify their therapeutic goals and encourage their clients to: (a) make changes in their inferences; (b) change the negative events in their lives; and (c) modify their behaviour so that they get some immediate benefit from the counselling process. However, rational-emotive counsellors do recognise that for the most part such clients are vulnerable to future disturbance because they have not addressed the core of their emotional and behavioural problems — that is, the musturbatory and dogmatic demands that they make about themselves, others, and the world. Thus, rational-emotive counsellors are willing to compromise and do not dogmatically insist that their

clients always work towards addressing and overcoming their musturbatory cognitions (Dryden, 1987a).

Whenever possible, however, rational-emotive counsellors strive
to encourage their clients to internalise the three major RET
insights that were outlined on p. 12. To reiterate, this means helping clients to acknowledge: (a) that past or present activating
events do not cause their disturbed emotional and behavioural
consequences — rather it is their irrational beliefs about these
activating events that largely create their disturbed feelings and
behaviours; (b) that irrespective of how they have disturbed themselves in the past, they now upset themselves largely because they
keep reindoctrinating themselves in the present with their irrational
beliefs; and (c) that although they are human and very easily, and
to some degree naturally, tend to disturb themselves by clinging to
their self-defeating thoughts, feelings, and actions, nevertheless
they can largely (but not totally) overcome their disturbances in the
long run. They can do this by working hard and repeatedly, both
to dispute their irrational beliefs and to counteract the effects of
these beliefs by strongly acting against them.

The Counselling Relationship
RET does not dogmatically insist that one specific kind of counselling relationship be established between counsellor and client;
indeed, rational-emotive counsellors are encouraged to be flexible
with respect to the kind of relationships they develop with different
clients. Nevertheless it is true to say that rational-emotive counsellors tend to favour establishing certain therapeutic conditions and
therapeutic styles with their clients.

Therapeutic conditions   As has been discussed above, one of the
most important goals that rational-emotive counsellors have is to
encourage their clients to accept themselves unconditionally as
fallible human beings who often act self-defeatingly but who are
never essentially good or bad. As such, rational-emotive counsellors
themselves strive to accept their clients unconditionally and try not
to denigrate their clients or dogmatically to insist that their clients
must behave in certain ways, either within or outside counselling
sessions. However, this does not prevent rational-emotive counsellors from bringing to the attention of their clients aspects of their
clients' behaviour which are self-defeating and impede the goals of
other people. Ideally, then, a counselling relationship is established
where both counsellor and client strive to accept self and other as
fallible. The preferred rational-emotive counselling relationship,
therefore, is an egalitarian one where both participants are equal

in their humanity, although unequal at the outset with respect to expertise and skills in personal problem solving.

Partly because of the egalitarian nature of the counselling relationship, rational-emotive counsellors strive to be as open as therapeutically desirable and do not refrain from giving highly personal information about themselves should their clients ask for it, except when they judge that their clients would use such information either against themselves or against their counsellors. However, such openness and the self-disclosure which accompanies it is encouraged for therapeutic purposes. Thus, when rational-emotive counsellors disclose that they have in the past experienced similar problems to their clients, it is not only to indicate to clients that they are on an equal footing as humans with their clients but also to teach their clients what they did to overcome these problems. In doing so rational-emotive counsellors serve as credible and encouraging role models. The basic message is: 'I am human too, I have experienced similar problems to you in the past, I overcame them and this is how I overcame them. Perhaps you can learn from my experience and take elements of it and apply this to your own problem-solving efforts.'

Ellis (1987a) has often noted that emotional disturbance incorporates an attitude where the person takes life *too* seriously. Given that, rational-emotive counsellors like to be appropriately humorous with their clients wherever possible. In doing so they demonstrate empathically and humorously to clients the comic aspects of their dogmatic irrational beliefs and teach their clients the therapeutic benefits of taking a serious but not overly serious attitude towards life. It is important to stress that this is done from a position of unconditional acceptance of clients and that when humorous interventions are employed, they are directed not at the clients themselves, but at their self-defeating thoughts, feelings, and actions. It should be noted, however, that some clients do not benefit from such humour and thus, again, the principle of therapeutic flexibility applies — vary your style of intervention to maximise your therapeutic relationships with different clients.

The world of counselling has been heavily influenced by the work of Carl Rogers (1957), and in particular his statements concerning the importance of certain core therapeutic conditions — that is, counsellor empathy, genuineness, and unconditional positive regard. Rational-emotive counsellors would agree with these, particularly the importance of unconditional acceptance and genuineness. With respect to empathy, rational-emotive counsellors offer their clients not only affective empathy — that is, communicating that they understand how their clients feel, but also philosophic empathy —

that is, showing them that they also understand the philosophies that underpin these feelings.

The one disagreement rational-emotive counsellors have with a large majority of counsellors from other therapeutic orientations concerns the role of counsellor warmth in the counselling process. Rational-emotive counsellors argue that offering clients unconditional acceptance is more important than offering them undue counsellor warmth. In RET the latter has two major risks. First, counsellor warmth may unwittingly reinforce clients' dire need for love and approval — an irrational belief which is believed to lie at the core of much psychological disturbance. Secondly, counsellor warmth may also unwittingly reinforce the philosophy of low frustration tolerance that many clients have. This is particularly the case if being warm means refraining from actively encouraging, and in some cases, strongly pushing clients to involve themselves in uncomfortable experiences for the long-term benefit of achieving therapeutic change.

Therapeutic Style   Ellis (1979a) recommends that rational-emotive counsellors adopt an active-directive therapeutic style with most clients. He argues that this style is important, particularly at the beginning of counselling in that it encourages clients to go quickly and efficiently to the philosophic core of their emotional and behavioural problems. However, as noted above, effective rational-emotive counsellors vary their therapeutic styles and can adopt a variety of styles to fit with the therapeutic requirements of different clients. Thus, for example, they would adopt: (a) a formal therapeutic style with clients who believe that effective counsellors should be business-like and expert; (b) a more informal style with clients who value interacting with a friendly and more personally involved counsellor; and (c) a tough no-nonsense style with clients who seem to benefit from such a therapeutic style. In addition, there may be indications for adopting different therapeutic styles with clients who have different personality styles. Thus, Beutler (1983) has argued that it is important to avoid developing an overly friendly, emotionally charged style of interaction with 'hysterical' clients, an overly intellectual style with obsessive-compulsive clients, and an overly directive style with clients who very easily retreat into passivity. However, much more research is needed on this question of therapeutic flexibility with respect to counsellor style in rational-emotive counselling before any more definitive statements can be made on this issue.

It is important to realise, as will be shown in Part 3, that the relationship between counsellor and client does change during the process of rational-emotive counselling, particularly with respect to the active-directive aspects of the counsellor's style. Thus, when rational-emotive counselling is effective, the counsellor increasingly encourages the client to assume more responsibility for therapeutic change and, correspondingly, the counsellor's level of directiveness fades. When this occurs, rational-emotive counsellors take a less directive prompting role, encouraging their clients to put into practice elements of the rational-emotive problem-solving method which they have increasingly used during the early and middle stages of counselling.

Emphasis on Disputing Irrational Beliefs

I argued earlier that rational-emotive theory adheres to the principle of psychological interactionism — namely, that beliefs, feelings, and behaviours cannot be separated from one another and in reality interact, often in quite complex ways. However, it is true that rational-emotive counsellors direct much of their therapeutic attention to helping clients to dispute their irrational beliefs, using cognitive, emotive, imaginal, and behavioural methods. This emphasis on disputing irrational beliefs involves the ability: (a) to detect the presence of such irrational beliefs; (b) to discriminate them from rational beliefs; and (c) to engage in a process called debating, whereby clients are encouraged to question how logical, consistent with reality, and pragmatic their irrational beliefs are. However, it should be noted once again that although cognitive disputing is a central component to rational-emotive counselling, it is by no means the only defining feature of this approach to counselling. I wish to underscore this because many critics, and indeed many researchers who have carried out empirical studies on rational-emotive therapy, seem to equate RET with its cognitive-restructuring aspects. Thus, while a central core of RET is helping clients to dispute their irrational beliefs and to replace these irrational philosophies with rational philosophies, this is done in many different ways, as will be shown below.

Multimodal Emphasis

Rational-emotive counsellors agree with Arnold Lazarus (1981) that it is important to take a multimodal approach to counselling. Thus, rational-emotive counsellors encourage their clients to use many cognitive, emotive-evocative, imaginal, and behavioural techniques in the pursuit of changing their irrational ideas. In addition, because RET stresses the biological as well as the environmental and social sources of human disturbance, rational-emotive counsellors favour both the use of medication where appropriate, and of physical techniques (including nutrition, exercise and relaxation methods) as an adjunct to the therapeutic process. However, such methods are used to encourage clients to work towards changing their irrational philosophies and are not used necessarily as an end in themselves.

Selective Eclecticism
Rational-emotive counselling is what I have called a theoretically consistent approach to eclecticism (Dryden, 1987b). This means that rational-emotive counsellors are encouraged to use a wide range of therapeutic techniques originated by counsellors from other therapeutic schools. However, in doing so they would not accept the theoretical principles advocated by these other theorists; rather, techniques are freely borrowed from other schools with the major purpose of encouraging clients to identify, challenge, and change their irrational beliefs. As such, RET de-emphasises the use of methods which discourage or impede clients from adopting a direct focus on changing their irrational ideologies. Thus, it avoids, although not in any absolute sense, using procedures that: (a) help people become more dependent — for example, the creation of a transference neurosis and the use of therapist as a strong reinforcer; (b) encourage clients to become more gullible and suggestible — for example, certain kinds of Pollyanna-ish positive-thinking methods; (c) are long-winded and inefficient — for example, free association and other psychoanalytic methods that discourage clients from focusing on their irrational beliefs; (d) help people to feel better in the short-term rather than to get better in the long-term — for example, some experiential techniques like getting in touch with and fully expressing one's feelings; (e) have dubious validity and have not received empirical support from research studies even though proponents claim great therapeutic success for these procedures (for example, neurolinguistic programming); (f) include anti-scientific and mystical philosophies (for example, faith healing and mysticism); and (g) appear to be harmful to a variety of clients — for example, encouraging clients, as in primal therapy, to scream, shout, and to express their angry feelings in an explosive manner.

It should be noted, however, that rational-emotive counsellors may use some of the above techniques for specific purposes. Thus, for example, experiential techniques can be used to help people to identify emotions prior to encouraging them to identify the irrational beliefs that underpin these emotions. Counsellor warmth may be warranted when clients are severely depressed; here the fact that the counsellor may show that he or she is very caring and concerned may inspire hope in such clients. In addition, Ellis (1985b) has argued that he may be prepared to use some of these inefficient techniques with clients as a last resort when all else has failed.

The Importance of Homework

Most rational-emotive counsellors see their clients for one hour a week. This means that for the remaining 167 hours in the week, their clients are on their own. This is a salutary reminder to those who claim that what goes on within counselling sessions has more therapeutic impact than what goes on between counselling sessions. Ellis has argued from RET's inception that clients who put into practice between sessions what they have learned within sessions will gain more from counselling than clients who steadfastly refuse to act on what they have learned in counselling sessions. Thus, for rational-emotive counsellors, encouraging clients to execute properly negotiated and well-designed homework assignments is considered to be a central part of the counselling process. Indeed, Ellis (1983a) and Persons et al. (1988) have reported empirical data to suggest that clients who carry out homework assignments in cognitively-oriented approaches to counselling achieve a better outcome than clients who do not execute such assignments. Therefore effective rational-emotive counsellors pay a lot of attention to the concept of homework in counselling, devoting sufficient time to discussing why this is a central part of the counselling process and to negotiating such assignments with their clients. In particular, they pay specific attention to factors which may discourage clients from successfully carrying out homework assignments and attempt to trouble-shoot such obstacles to psychotherapeutic change.

Confronting and Overcoming Obstacles to Change

I mentioned directly above that an important aspect of rational-emotive counselling concerns identifying and overcoming obstacles to therapeutic change that arise when clients attempt to execute homework assignments. However, obstacles to change pervade the entire counselling process, and given this clinical fact, rational-emotive counsellors attempt to engage their clients in a co-operative exploration concerning the nature of these obstacles. If the obstacles to change can be attributed to the clients, counsellors will first identify the irrational beliefs that underpin their resistant behaviour. This having been done, counsellors urge their clients to overcome these obstacles so that they do not unduly interfere with the nature of therapeutic change.

Obstacles to change can occur: (a) within the counselling relationship; (b) within the client; and (c) within the counsellor. When obstacles to change occur within the counselling relationship it may be that the particular match between counsellor and client is not a good one. The best way of handling this may be a judicious referral to a different rational-emotive counsellor. In addition, it has to be acknowledged that some clients do not find rational-emotive counselling a helpful therapeutic method and may well do better with a different approach to counselling. This is because the ideas central to rational-emotive counselling — namely, that one's emotional disturbance is determined by one's presently held irrational beliefs and that one has to work and practise to overcome one's emotional and behavioural problems — are at variance with the beliefs of the client and no amount of counsellor intervention may change the client's mind on these points. Here, a judicious referral to a counsellor from a different school may be indicated.

However, relationship obstacles to change can occur because the counsellor has unwittingly adopted a therapeutic style which is implicitly reinforcing the client's difficulties. Thus, the counsellor may be offering the client too much warmth and inadvertently reinforcing the client's need for approval, or the counsellor may be adopting an overly directive style of interaction which encourages an already passive client to become more passive both in the counselling situation and in everyday life. It is important for counsellors to monitor their style of participation and to ask themselves continually whether their therapeutic style is encouraging or discouraging their clients from changing.

The second source of obstacles to therapeutic change resides in clients themselves, an issue which will be discussed further in Part 3. However, it should be noted here that clients may have irrational beliefs about certain aspects of the rational-emotive counselling process which may discourage them from changing. In particular, they may well have a philosophy of low frustration tolerance towards taking major responsibility for effecting their own improvement. Thus, they may believe that they should not be expected to work hard in counselling and that doing so is too difficult and too uncomfortable. It is important that counsellors encourage their clients to identify, challenge, and change such impeding philosophies if the latter are to benefit from rational-emotive counselling in the long-term.

Rational-emotive counsellors are by no means immune from their own self-defeating beliefs, which may well serve as obstacles to the change process. Ellis (1983b) has outlined five major counsellor irrational beliefs that may serve as obstacles to client change:

1 I have to be successful with all of my clients practically all of the time.

2   I must be an outstanding counsellor, clearly better than other counsellors that I know or hear about.
3   I have to be greatly respected and loved by all my clients.
4   Since I am doing my best and working so hard as a counsellor, my clients must be equally hard working and responsible, must listen to me carefully, and must always push themselves to change.
5   Because I'm a person in my own right, I must be able to enjoy myself during counselling sessions and to use these sessions to solve my personal problems as much as to help clients with their difficulties.

The presence of these beliefs may lead counsellors to back off from strongly encouraging their clients to change when this is appropriate, or to become inappropriately involved with their clients in a manner that side-tracks rational-emotive counselling from its problem-solving focus. It is thus important for rational-emotive counsellors to monitor their work regularly, to be prepared to accept themselves fully when they discover that they are side-tracking the counselling process inappropriately, and, when this is the case, to identify, challenge, and change the irrational beliefs that have produced the side-tracks. It is also important for counsellors to seek supervision of their work, since it may be that supervisors may be able to spot additional instances which may indicate that counsellors' own irrational beliefs have come to the fore and are serving as an obstacle to client change.

Force and Energy in Therapeutic Change

The theory of RET holds that when clients are emotionally disturbed they tend to cling very forcefully and energetically to their main irrational beliefs, and that even when they have 'insight' into these beliefs they may still strongly believe them and refuse to give them up. In such circumstances, rational-emotive counsellors are not loathe to engage their clients in a very forceful and energetic process of disputing their irrational beliefs and to encourage them to intervene very forcefully, vividly and energetically when they are disputing their own irrational beliefs (Ellis, 1979b). Thus, force and energy can be brought to the entire range of cognitive, imaginal, and behavioural assignments. This latter point serves to remind critics that rational-emotive counselling does stress the emotive aspects of counselling and does bring passion to the counselling process. Without this focus on force and energy, clients will tend to challenge their irrational beliefs weakly and insipidly, and will thus experience very little benefit.

Characteristics of Effective Rational-Emotive Counsellors
In my experience as a trainer in RET over the last decade, I have
noticed that effective rational-emotive counsellors demonstrate the
following qualities:

1   They are vitally interested in helping their clients.
2   They demonstrate an unconditional acceptance of their clients
    as fallible human beings but are not loathe to confront their
    clients with their self-defeating behaviour.
3   They use a wide range of therapeutic techniques spawned from
    other schools but do so in a way consistent with the clinical
    theory of rational-emotive counselling.
4   They demonstrate high frustration tolerance when clients do not
    change as quickly as they would like, adopt a problem-solving
    focus throughout counselling and do not use the counselling
    process for their own personal indulgence or to meet their own
    neurotic needs; in this regard they are neither under-involved
    nor over-involved with their clients.

Ellis (1987b) has argued that effective rational-emotive counsellors
have the additional following characteristics: (a) they enjoy being
active and directive; (b) they are devoted to philosophy, science,
logic and empiricism; (c) they are skilled teachers and communica-
tors; (d) they unconditionally accept themselves for their therapeutic errors and work towards minimising these errors in the
future; (e) they enjoy problem-solving; (f) they are experimental
and take appropriate risks in the counselling process; (g) they have
a good sense of humour which they use appropriately in counselling;
(h) they are energetic and forceful; and (i) they apply rational-
emotive counselling in a way that is consistent with its clinical theory
but in a flexible and non-dogmatic manner.

In this first part of the book I have outlined the basic principles
of rational-emotive counselling. In particular I have discussed the
theory that underpins its practice and I have discussed the key
elements of this approach to counselling in action. In Part 2 I will
outline the rational-emotive counselling sequence, and in the final
part I will consider the process of rational-emotive counselling from
beginning to end.

Notes

   1 For a full discussion of Ellis's arguments concerning the biological basis of
human irrationality, see Ellis (1976).
   2 Some RET counsellors prefer to include only events or imaginary events that
may occur under A, grouping all cognitive activity including inferences under B.
   3 Helping clients to achieve a profound philosophic change is a topic which is
beyond the scope of this book, which focuses on short-term counselling.

PART 2   THE RATIONAL-EMOTIVE COUNSELLING SEQUENCE

In this part, I will first give a brief overview of the rational-emotive counselling sequence. Secondly, I will introduce my client, 'Steve', whose case illustrates rational-emotive counselling in action throughout this book. Finally, I will discuss the steps in the rational-emotive counselling sequence using my work with Steve to demonstrate each step in action.

Throughout this part of the book I shall address you, the reader, directly and shall assume that you are dealing with your client's emotional problems one at a time. Thus, in specifying the rational-emotive counselling sequence I will assume that you are working with a *given* client problem.[1]

An Overview of the Rational-Emotive Counselling Sequence

In this section I will provide a brief overview of the rational-emotive counselling sequence (which is summarised in Figure 2). I will consider each step separately throughout the rest of Part 2.

As will be discussed in Part 3 the initial stage of rational-emotive counselling often involves first, greeting your client[2], secondly, helping him to express his concerns, and thirdly, discussing his expectations for counselling and agreeing basic practicalities (for example, fees). After you have done this I suggest that you adopt a problem-solving attitude at the outset, and ask your client which problem he would like to discuss with you first. If necessary, and particularly when your client lists several problems, encourage him to focus on one and work towards an agreement concerning the nature of this problem. At this point you might ask your client what he would like to achieve as a consequence of discussing this problem.

After you have defined the problem and agreed with your client that you will both address yourselves to this problem, you are ready to carry out an assessment of the problem, breaking it down into its ABC components. You may first either assess A (the activating event, including the client's inferences about the event) or C (the

Step 1:   Ask for a problem

Step 2:   Define and agree the target problem
                 (set goals in line with problem as defined)

Step 3:   Assess C

Step 4:   Assess A   Assess the
                                                       target
Step 5:   Determine whether or not your client has a   problem
                 secondary emotional problem   (set goals
                    (and assess if appropriate)   in line with
                                                         the problem
Step 6:   Teach the B–C connection   as assessed)

Step 7:   Assess iB

Step 8:   Connect iB and C

Step 9:   Dispute iB

Step 10:   Prepare your client to deepen his conviction in his
                         rational beliefs

Step 11:   Homework: encourage your client to put his new
                      learning into practice

Step 12:   Check homework assignments

Step 13:   Facilitate the working-through process

A = Activating event (and inference)
B = Belief
iB = Irrational belief
C = Emotion

Figure 2 *The rational-emotive counselling sequence*

emotional and behavioural consequences of the client's evaluative
beliefs about A). If you decide to assess A first, then go on to assess
C. Conversely if you decide to assess C first, then go on to assess
A. Help your client to understand that A does not cause C but that
there is a missing step, namely that his disturbed feelings are largely
determined by his irrational evaluative beliefs (B) about A. At this
stage, or earlier if it is appropriate, you may check whether your
client also has a secondary emotional problem — that is, an

emotional problem about his original (that is, primary) problem. By a secondary emotional problem is meant, for example, depression about being depressed, anxious about being afraid, guilty about being angry, ashamed about being jealous, and so on. Thus, the client's primary emotional problem becomes an activating event for an irrational belief which in turn results in the secondary emotional problem. If he does have a secondary emotional problem and particularly where it significantly interferes with his original emotional problem, agree that this will now become the focus for discussion. You can then carry out an assessment of this secondary problem using the ABC framework.

Whatever problem (primary or secondary) you are now assessing, and assuming that you have correctly assessed A and C and helped the client to understand that it is B that largely determines C rather than A, you are now in a position to assess your client's irrational beliefs. While you are doing this, help your client to discriminate keenly between his irrational and rational beliefs. The next step is to help your client to understand the relationship between his inappropriate negative emotion(s) at C and his irrational beliefs at B. When the client has understood this connection and can see that in order to overcome his emotional problem at C he needs to change his irrational beliefs at B, you are now in a position to help the client to dispute his irrational beliefs.

During the disputing process you may use pragmatic, logical, and empirical arguments. The purpose of disputing is to help the client understand why his irrational beliefs are self-defeating, illogical, and empirically inconsistent with reality, and why the alternative rational beliefs are self-enhancing, logical, and realistic. Once your client has understood this, you are now in a position to encourage him to consider ways in which he can put his understanding into practice.

Once the client has learned that gaining conviction in the new rational beliefs involves practice, you can negotiate appropriate homework assignments. The purpose of homework assignments is to help your client translate his knowledge (intellectual insight) into conviction (emotional insight). It is very important for you to check on your client's experiences in carrying out homework assignments. In particular it is important to trouble-shoot any obstacles to change that your client identifies.

When your client has made some progress, encourage him to practise his new rational beliefs in different contexts using different cognitive, emotive, and behavioural techniques. In this way your client will be able to integrate his new rational beliefs into his emotional and behavioural repertoire.

Having reviewed the rational-emotive counselling sequence I

shall now discuss each step in greater detail. But first let me introduce Steve, my client. I will describe my work with him throughout this book to illustrate rational-emotive counselling in action.

Introducing Steve

When I first saw him, Steve was a 26-year-old white Jewish man who was referred to me by one of his friends, whom I had counselled a few months earlier. Steve was in his third year of a PhD course in economics at one of the colleges in London University. He was the only child of non-orthodox Jewish parents whom he described as caring and encouraging. He had a fiancée who worked as a social worker and they planned to get married as soon as Steve had finished his PhD. He had never sought counselling before.

Step 1: Ask for a Problem

After you have greeted your client and dealt with certain practicalities (for example, fees), adopt a problem-focused stance at the outset. Asking your client what problem he would like to discuss first (referred to here as the target problem) communicates to him a number of messages. First, it emphasises that you are both there to get a job done — that is, to help the client to overcome his emotional problems. Secondly, it illustrates that RET is an efficient and focused approach to emotional problem solving. Thirdly, it indicates that as a counsellor you are going to be active and to direct your client immediately to a discussion of his problems.

Two Strategies: Client Choice vs. Client's Most Serious Problem

There are two basic strategies you can adopt when asking your client to focus on a target problem. The first concerns client choice. Here you ask your client to choose a particular problem that he wishes to discuss first (for example, 'What would you like to work on first?'). This may or may not be his most serious problem. The second strategy is to ask your client to start with his most serious problem. Here, for example, you might ask: 'What are you most bothered about in your life right now?'

When your Client does not Immediately Identify a Target Problem

What can you do if your client does not immediately identify anything to work on? First, remind your client that he does not have to choose a serious problem. Tell him that it is perfectly in order to start the process with an issue that is impeding him in some slight way. Remind him that there is always something human beings can work on since we usually operate at a mode of functioning that is less than optimal. Encourage your client to identify *feelings* or *behaviours* that he would like to decrease or *feelings* or *behaviours* that he would like to increase.

When your client does not immediately disclose a problem, an indirect way of identifying one is to ask him what he would like to achieve from counselling. When your client articulates his goal you could then ask him for ways in which he is not presently achieving this goal. This may well lead to a discussion of possible feelings and/ or behaviours that your client may identify as serving to impede him from achieving his goal. You should then explore these factors further without necessarily labelling them as 'problems'. This is an important point. The word 'problem' serves to discourage some clients from becoming engaged in a problem-focused therapy like RET. If this is the case, use a term which is more acceptable to your client, one that helps him to engage in RET.

When the Nature of your Client's Problem is Clear, and when it is not

It is frequently obvious what the nature of your client's problem is at this stage, and when this is the case you may proceed to assess it.

However, when the nature of your client's target problem is not clear then you are advised to come to an agreed definition of it with your client (see step 2) before proceeding to the assessment stage. Also, when your client has disclosed a number of problems, then it is important to agree with your client which one you are both going to work on first (that is, the target problem). If its nature is clear proceed to assess it (steps 3–7); if not, proceed to step 2. When your client has several problems, remember to work on one problem at a time. After you finish all the steps for problem 1, then go back and repeat the steps for problem 2 and so on.

Step 1: Steve

First, I greeted Steve and found out how he came to be referred to me. Then we discussed his expectations for counselling and agreed a fee appropriate to his situation. I then asked him what problem he would like to start with. He said that he had fallen behind in his work and was using every excuse to avoid focusing on his PhD thesis. He disclosed that he did not get on with his PhD supervisor, whom he considered had treated him in a cavalier manner by not giving his work serious attention. On enquiry, Steve said that he had never mentioned this to his supervisor because he was scared to disclose his feelings. He was also very angry towards the supervisor. As a consequence of these feelings he had stopped handing in work to the supervisor, who had not reacted to this new state of affairs.

I noted that Steve had several problems, and suggested that we list them so that we could deal with them one by one. Steve agreed and we developed the following list:

1 procrastination;
2 anger towards supervisor;
3 anxiety about confronting supervisor.

I again asked Steve which problem he would like to start with and he chose 'procrastination'.

Step 2: Define and Agree upon the Target Problem

Arriving at a common understanding with your client concerning the nature of his problem, and agreeing to work on this problem, is an important step in RET in that it strengthens the therapeutic alliance at the outset. It enables you and your client to work as a team and it helps your client to feel understood and to have confidence that you know what you are doing.

Distinguish between an Emotional Problem and a Practical Problem

As Bard (1980) has noted, RET is a method of counselling which helps clients to overcome their *emotional* problems and is not designed to help them at first to overcome their *practical* problems directly, and it is important to help your client to understand this distinction. Of course, clients often have emotional problems about their practical problems and these will become the focus for therapeutic exploration rather than the practical problems themselves. Also in RET, as clients' emotional problems are addressed, their practical problems may be dealt with, too (Ellis, 1985b).

Target Inappropriate (but not Appropriate) Negative Emotions for Change

In Part 1, I distinguished between inappropriate and appropriate negative emotions. Do not encourage your client to change his appropriate negative emotions since these are healthy reactions to negative life events which will help your client to come to terms with or to change the situation. However, do target for change feelings which stem from irrational beliefs — that is, inappropriate negative emotions. Help your client to understand the difference between these two types of negative emotions. The question 'How is this a problem for you?' will often lead to a useful discussion and help you and your client to identify and define a 'real' emotional problem.

Select One Problem (the Target Problem) if Several are Disclosed

If your client discloses a number of problems, it is very important for you to come to an agreement with him concerning which problem you are both going to address first. As already discussed in step 1, this might be the problem that the client wishes to work on first or, if this different, one which he regards as most serious. The most important factor to consider here is that you and your client agree upon a particular working focus.

Operationalise Vague Problems

When your client discusses his target problem in vague or confusing terms, it is important to help him to operationalise the problem. Thus, for example, if your client says: 'My wife is a pain in the ass', it is important to help him to specify what this statement means in operational terms — for example: 'What is it that your wife does that leads you to conclude that she is a pain in the ass, and how do you feel when she acts in this way?' If you do this you will find that you are beginning to formulate the problem in ABC terms. The practical problem is the wife's behaviour which makes her a 'pain in the ass'; the emotional problem is the disturbed, inappropriate emotion your client feels when the wife acts in this way.

Focus on Helping your Client Change C, not A

A common difficulty that you may face at this point is that your client may wish to change A rather than his feelings (C) about A. Changing A is a practical solution; changing C is the emotional solution. If you do encounter this difficulty you can use a number of strategies to encourage your client to change C before attempting to change A. First, you can help your client to see that he can change A more effectively if he is not emotionally disturbed (at C) about it.

Secondly, it may be that your client already knows how to change A but cannot at present do so. If this is the case, it is important to help him to understand that the reason why he cannot use his productive problem-solving strategies to change A is probably due to the fact that he is emotionally disturbed about A.

Thirdly, if your client does not yet have productive problem-solving strategies in his repertoire to change A, you can often encourage him to focus on his problems at C by showing him that he will learn such strategies more effectively if he is not emotionally disturbed about A.

When You have still not Identified a Problem

If at this stage you have still not reached an agreement with your client concerning the nature of his problem, you can suggest to your client that he keep a problem diary. Encourage your client to monitor his disturbed feelings during the following week and suggest that he make written notes of what these feelings were, and when and where he experienced them.

Step 2: Steve

Remember that Steve wanted to deal with his procrastination first. I asked him to tell me a little more about this problem and the following dialogue ensued.

> *Steve*: Well, I find that I can't settle down to any work. I put all my papers in order but I just use any excuse to distract myself. I make myself endless cups of coffee. I telephone friends and I even tidy up my study even though I'm not noted for my tidiness.
>
> *Windy*: But let's suppose that you did sit down and start to work, what feelings do you think you might experience?
>
> *Steve*: I don't know. I never get that far these days.
>
> *Windy*: But let's suppose that you did. Let your imagination go and see if you can get a sense of the feelings that you might experience.
>
> *Steve*: OK . . . [*pause*] . . . I guess I'd really feel uncomfortable. My mind would race and I'd start to move around.
>
> *Windy*: And what would you do then?
>
> *Steve*: Oh I'd stop working.
>
> *Windy*: So could it be that what you call procrastination is in some way related to you avoiding those uncomfortable feelings that you predict you would experience if you did start working?
>
> *Steve*: I'd never thought about it like that but, yes, I think you're right.
>
> *Windy*: So since you want to get over your procrastination problem does it make sense to focus more on those negative feelings and see what they're related to so that you can get yourself into a better state of mind to work?
>
> *Steve*: Yes, that's certainly a reasonable way of going about things.

My hypothesis was that Steve's procrastination could be considered to be a form of avoidance behaviour; such behaviour serving to help him avoid negative feelings. This initial hypothesis seemed to be supported by what Steve said to me. My further hunch (which I explore under step 3) was that these were negative inappropriate feelings of anxiety.

Assess the Target Problem

I will now assume that you have selected a target problem with your client and that you both broadly understand its nature. The next stage is to assess the problem.

Be specific

During the assessment process, it is important for you to be as specific as you can. Your client experiences his emotional problem and holds related irrational beliefs in *specific* contexts and, as such, being specific will help you to obtain reliable and valid data about A, B, and C. It is often helpful to give your client a plausible rationale for your specificity, especially if he tends to discuss his target problem in vague terms. Help him to understand that being specific about his problem will encourage him to deal more constructively with it in the situations about which he is disturbed.

A good way of modelling specificity for your client is for you to ask for a recent or a typical example of the target problem, such as, 'When was the last time A happened?'

If your client has difficulty in providing you with a specific example of the target problem, this *may* be because he has a secondary emotional problem about his primary emotional problem (for example, shame). If you suspect that this is the case, do not assume that you are correct: test your hypothesis.

Step 3: Assess C

I noted earlier in the overview of the rational-emotive counselling sequence that you may assess A before C or C before A, depending upon which element of the target problem your client raises first during the assessment process. I shall first consider the assessment of C.

Check again that You are Dealing with a Negative Inappropriate Emotion

When you begin to assess C, remember that your client's emotional problem will be an *inappropriate* disturbed negative emotion, not an *appropriate* non-disturbed negative emotion (see Table 1, p. 11). In Table 1 I used specific terms for both negative inappropriate and negative appropriate emotions. An inappropriate disturbed negative emotion differs from an appropriate non-disturbed negative emotion in that the inappropriate emotion: (a) usually involves a great deal of emotional pain; (b) often motivates one to behave in a self-defeating manner; and (c) blocks one from achieving one's goals. Please note, however, that these words refer to distinctions made in RET theory and may not necessarily correspond to the way your clients use those words. Thus, for example, your client may talk about anxiety but may actually experience concern and vice versa (see Dryden, 1986 for an extended discussion of this issue). It is important that you identify a negative inappropriate emotion and that you and your client use similar language when referring to this emotion. You may either encourage your client to adopt the RET terminology of emotions or you may choose to adopt the client's use of feeling language. But whatever course you take, be consistent in your vocabulary throughout counselling.

Focus on an Emotional C

Note that C can be emotional or behavioural. However, because dysfunctional behaviours are often defensive in nature and often exist to help clients avoid experiencing certain inappropriate negative emotions, I will encourage you in this book to restrict C to negative inappropriate *emotions*. Thus, if your client wishes to stop smoking, regard this as a defensive behaviour and encourage him to identify emotions that he might experience were he to refrain from smoking. I suggest that you also adopt this strategy if your client mentions that his problem is procrastination or some other kind of avoidance behaviour (as I did with Steve in step 2).

Clarify C

If your client identifies a vague or unclear C there are a number of specific techniques that you can use to clarify the nature of this C. Thus, you can use a number of Gestalt exercises like the empty chair technique (see Passons, 1975) and Gendlin's (1978) focusing technique, and imagery methods where you ask your client to imagine an example of his problem and to identify any associated feelings. When his clients experience difficulty in identifying a specific emotion, Albert Ellis encourages them to 'Take a wild guess', a method which surprisingly yields quite useful information about C.

Frustration is an A not a C

Your client may talk about feeling frustrated at C. Some RET therapists prefer to regard frustration as an activating event rather than a feeling (Trexler, 1976). As a C, frustration in RET theory is usually regarded as an *appropriate* negative emotion experienced by your client when his goals are blocked. However, when your client says that he feels frustrated, he may be referring to a negative *inappropriate* emotion. One way of telling whether your client's feeling of frustration is an inappropriate or an appropriate negative emotion is to ask him whether or not the feeling is bearable. If he says that it is unbearable then it may very well be that your client is experiencing a negative inappropriate emotion and it is thus a target for change.

Assess your Client's Motivation to Change C
Assess your client's understanding of the dysfunctionality or self-defeating nature of the target emotion (C). Sometimes clients experience inappropriate disturbed negative emotions which they are not motivated to change. This lack of motivation results when your client, while experiencing distress and pain, does not recognise the destructive nature of the emotion he is experiencing. This happens most frequently with anger, and sometimes occurs with guilt and depression. If your client does not recognise why his emotion is inappropriate, I recommend that you spend as much time as necessary helping him to understand this point. Basically, this can be accomplished in three steps. First, help your client to assess the consequences of the inappropriate emotion. What happens when he feels that way? Does he act constructively? Does he act self-defeatingly? Does he stop himself from acting appropriately?

Secondly, point out to him that the goal is to replace the inappropriate emotion with the corresponding appropriate emotion. Sometimes this is difficult since your client may have rigid ideas about the way he is supposed to feel. Usually, however, he will be able to conceptualise that one can experience the appropriate emotion in a given situation if he can be provided with suitable models.

Finally, assess what the consequences would be if he felt the appropriate emotion in the same situation. Since he has probably not done this, help him to imagine how he would act and what the different outcomes would be if he did experience the appropriate emotion in the context of the same activating event. Compare the outcomes to both the inappropriate and appropriate emotions. Your client will usually understand the advantages of the appropriate emotion and this will increase his motivation to change C.

Avoid the Following Pitfalls while Assessing C
There are a number of pitfalls to avoid while assessing your client's problematic emotions at C. First, do not ask questions that reinforce the 'A causes C' connection. Novice rational-emotive counsellors frequently ask their clients questions such as: 'How does *it* make you feel?' An alternative question which does not imply that A causes C is: 'How do you feel about it?'

Secondly, do not accept vague statements of feeling, such as 'bad', 'upset', 'miserable', and so on. When your client uses such vague terms help him to clarify exactly what he felt at C, and I again refer you to Table 1 which you can use as a guide to making discriminations among negative inappropriate emotions. In addition, do not accept statements such as 'I feel trapped', or 'I feel rejected', as referring to emotions at C. Recognise that we do not have a feeling called rejection or trapped; these terms refer to combinations of A, B, and C factors, and it is important to distinguish among the three during the assessment process. Thus, for example, if your client says: 'I felt rejected', help him to recognise that he may have been rejected at A. Then ask how he felt about that rejection at point C. Remember that it is important to break down such statements into their component parts and to ensure that your client's C statements do actually refer to emotions.

Step 3: Steve
Having established that Steve's procrastination served as behaviour that helped him to ward off uncomfortable negative feelings, my next task was to help us both to understand more clearly the nature of these negative feelings:

Windy: If you were to sit down and work and really let yourself experience those negative feelings, what kind of feelings would they be?

Steve: Upset feelings.

Windy: Yes, but what kind of upset feelings: upset anxious; upset angry; upset depressed or what?

Steve: Oh anxiety, definitely.

Windy: And presumably not the kind of anxiety that motivates performance?

Steve: No, certainly not.

Windy: So would you like to change these feelings?

Steve: Well, I'd like to get down to work again.

Windy: Right, but since your feelings of anxiety are preventing you from doing that, does it make sense to find out what they relate to so you can change them to feelings that will help you to work?

Steve: Yes, that makes sense.

It did not appear that Steve had any reservations about changing his anxious feelings. However, note that his main motivation was to resume his studying. Although he had agreed that focusing on and clarifying his negative feelings would be a good strategy in step 2, I had to deal with this issue again here in step 3 — namely, that we needed to help him overcome his anxiety first before he could overcome his procrastination.

Step 4: Assess A^3

Be Specific
As with assessments of C, when you assess A be as specific as you can. Thus, ask for the last time A occurred, a typical example of A, or the most relevant example that your client can recall.

Identify the Part of A that Triggered B
While you are assessing A, help your client to identify the most relevant part of A (that is, the part of A that triggered your client's irrational belief at B). As I include your client's inferences as part of A, it is important to recognise that your client's inferences are often chained (or linked) together. So assess this chain with the purpose of identifying the most relevant link of the chain — that is, the aspect of A which triggered your client's irrational beliefs at B, which in turn accounted for his problematic feelings at C. You can do this by using a technique called inference chaining — a procedure which helps you to identify how your client's inferences are linked.

Let us consider an example. Imagine that your client is anxious at point C. Your first enquiry concerning what he is anxious about reveals that he is due to give a class presentation. Now your task is to find out what it is about giving a class presentation that is anxiety-provoking in your client's mind. You can proceed as follows:

> *Counsellor*: What is it about giving the presentation that you are anxious about?
> *Client*: Well, I may not do a very good job.
> *Counsellor*: Let's assume for the moment that you don't. What's anxiety-provoking in your mind about that?
> *Client*: Well, if I don't do a good job in class then my teacher will give me a poor grade.
> *Counsellor*: Let's assume that as well. What would you be anxious about there?
> *Client*: That I might flunk the course.
> *Counsellor*: And if you did?
> *Client*: Oh my God, I couldn't face my father.
> *Counsellor*: So, if you told your father that you had failed what would be anxiety-provoking about that in your mind?
> *Client*: I can just see my father now, he would be devastated.
> *Counsellor*: And how would you feel if that happened?
> *Client*: Oh my God, that would be terrible, I really couldn't stand to see my father cry, I'd feel so very sorry for him.

Remember that your client was initially anxious about giving a class presentation. However, on further exploration, both the C and the A have changed. Initially the A was 'giving a class presentation' and the C was 'anxiety'. Using inference chaining you have now identified the A as 'seeing my father devastated by the news of my failure' and the C is other-pity. You will, of course, wish to know whether or not the new A is the most relevant one, that is, the one that triggered his irrational belief that determined his feelings at C.

One way to determine this is to write down the inference chain and review it with your client. Ask him to look at the chain and identify which aspect of the chain, particularly that which concerns A, is the most relevant for his particular problem. Another way of finding out whether the new A is the most relevant is to manipulate aspects of A and check your client's responses at C. In the above example, for example, you might say to your client: 'Let's suppose that you told your father and he wasn't devastated, in fact he could cope quite well with the news, would that have any impact on your anxiety about giving the class presentation?' If the client states that it would, you may be more confident that you have assessed the problem correctly. However, if your client states that he would still be anxious, given this change in A, then it is clear that seeing his father distressed (at A) and feeling very sorry for his father (at C) is not the most important aspect of your client's anxiety problem.[4]

To review, then, the purpose of inference chaining is to help the client to identify the most relevant aspect of A. When you have done this it is important to assess what your client's feelings are about this A since it may have changed. In the above example, the client first reported feeling anxious and then other-pity. Although this is complicated, you can either deal with your client's anxiety about the *prospect* of his father being devastated at the news of failure, or you can deal with his feelings of other-pity, once you have assumed that the new A (that is, the father being 'devastated') has happened. The point to remember here is that your main goal is to assess the most relevant part of A. This example also shows that your client's emotions, as well as his inferences, can be linked together.

A can Refer to Many Things

It is important for you to keep in mind that A might be an event, a thought, an inference, an image, a sensation, a behaviour, as well as an actual activating event.

Note, therefore, that your client's feelings at C may also serve as an A and he may well have a new set of troublesome feelings about his original feelings (referred to here as a secondary emotional problem). Thus, for example, your client may feel guilty (at C). This guilt may serve as a new A and your client may feel ashamed (new C) about feeling guilty. As noted elsewhere in this part of the book, it is important to keep in mind that your client may have a secondary emotional problem about his primary emotional problem, but this is not *always* the case. The existence of secondary emotional problems requires careful and open-minded assessment.

Assume Temporarily that A is True

When you assess A you may discover that your client's most relevant A is clearly distorted. If this is the case you may be tempted to dispute A. Resist this temptation. Rather, encourage your client to assume *temporarily* that A is correct. In the above example, it is not important at this stage to determine whether or not your client's father will become devastated when he tells him about flunking his class. What is important is to encourage your client to assume that A is correct, so as to help him to identify more accurately his irrational beliefs about this possibly distorted A which led to his feelings at point C.

Avoid the Following Pitfalls while Assessing A

There are a number of pitfalls to avoid while assessing A. First, do not obtain too much detail about it. When your client does give you a lot of detail, try to *abstract* the salient theme from what he says, or summarise what you understand to be the major aspect of A about which he may be emotionally disturbed. If you allow your client to talk at length about A, this discourages both of you from retaining a problem-solving approach to helping your client overcome his emotional difficulties. If this happens, interrupt your client tactfully and re-establish a specific focus. Thus, for example, you could say to your client: 'I think you may be giving me more detail than I require; what was it about this situation that you were most upset about?'

Secondly, discourage your client from describing A in vague terms. As noted above, get as clear and as specific an example of A as you can.

Since in RET it is important for you to work on one A at a time, a third pitfall occurs when your client talks about several 'A's. When this happens encourage your client to deal with the A which he considers to best illustrate the context in which he makes himself disturbed. Also, explain that you will deal with the other 'A's at a later date.

When You have still not Identified a Clear A

If at this stage your client has not identified a clear A, encourage him to keep a diary of activating events about which he makes himself disturbed during the time before his next session.

Step 4: Steve

Windy: OK, so let's see what you're anxious about. Imagine that you're sitting down and trying to work. Your mind is racing and you're fidgeting around. Now what do you think you would be anxious about?

Steve: I'd be anxious that my work wouldn't be creative enough.

Windy: In whose opinion?

Steve: That's a good question . . . [*pause*] . . . I think my supervisor's. Yeah, my supervisor.

Windy: OK. So let's assume for a moment that your supervisor wouldn't think your work wasn't very creative. [*Inference 1*] What would be anxiety-provoking in your mind about that?

Steve: Well, it would remind me that I may not get my PhD.

Windy: Well, that may or may not be true. People do get PhDs without showing that much creativity. But again let's assume that you're correct, and you wouldn't be awarded a PhD. [*Inference 2*] What would be anxiety-provoking in your mind about that?

Steve: Well, I wouldn't be able to get a top job in the City. [*Inference 3*]

Windy: Again let's assume that you're right. What would be anxiety-provoking about not getting a top job in the City?

Steve: Well, wait a minute, that's not the main thing. I guess it's the failure thing. I've never been able to contemplate failure and every time I try to focus on my work nowadays the thought that I might fail comes to mind.

Windy: So it's not so much your supervisor's opinion of your creativity *per se*, nor not getting a top job in the City. It's the thought of failing that you're most scared about. Is that it?

Steve: Yeah. That's it.

Agree on Goals

I have already stressed that it is important for you and your client to develop a common understanding concerning the nature of your client's target problem. I also advocate that you develop a similar understanding concerning your client's goals for change, and for a similar reason. Doing so facilitates a therapeutic alliance between you and your client.

When to Agree on Goals

If you look at Figure 2 (see p. 26) you will see that there are two occasions when you may wish to assess your client's goals for change. The first is when you define and agree your client's target problem. Here I suggest that you help your client to set a goal that is in line with the problem as defined. If, for example, your client's target problem is that he is overweight, his goal may be to achieve and maintain a specific target weight.

The second occasion when you may fruitfully assess your client's goal is at the assessment stage. Here the goal may be different.

Taking the above example, after you have agreed that your client's goal is to achieve and maintain a specific weight, your assessment of his overeating problem might indicate that he overeats when he is bored and that he gets anxious when he is bored. At this stage your client's goal would be: to deal more appropriately with the feeling of boredom so that he does not eat food as an inappropriate coping strategy. Thus, you may encourage your client to feel concerned (rather than anxious) about being bored and to use that feeling of concern to deal with boredom in more constructive ways. Thus, at the assessment stage encourage your client to select a negative appropriate emotion as his goal for change. Help him to understand why this is a realistic and constructive response to a negative activating event at A.

Help your Client to Take a Long-term Perspective when Agreeing on Goals
When discussing goals with your client, keep in mind the distinction between long- and short-term goals. Your client may choose a short-term goal that may in the long term be self-defeating and therefore irrational. Help your client to take a longer-term perspective and obtain a commitment that he will work towards his long-term productive goals.

Avoid the Following Pitfalls when Agreeing on Goals
First, do not accept your client's goals where he states that he wishes to experience 'less' of a negative inappropriate emotion — for example, 'I want to feel less anxious', or 'I want to feel less guilty'. According to rational-emotive theory, the presence of a negative inappropriate emotion — for example, anxiety or guilt — indicates that your client is holding an irrational belief, albeit in a less intense manner. As such you are again advised to help your client to distinguish between the negative inappropriate emotion in question, and that which is negative but appropriate to the situation. Encourage him to set the latter as his goal. Thus, he can choose to feel concerned instead of anxious and choose to feel sorry about breaking his moral code instead of guilty (self-downing) about himself for this violation.

Secondly, do not accept feeling goals which indicate that your client wishes to feel neutral, indifferent, or calm about events about which it would be rational for him to feel a negative appropriate emotion. Emotions indicating indifference, such as calmness when an unfortunate event occurs, indicate that your client does not have a rational belief about the event in question, whereas in reality he probably does prefer the event not to happen. If you go along with your client's goal to feel calm or indifferent about a negative event, you will encourage him to deny the existence of his desires rather than to think rationally.

Thirdly, for similar reasons, do not accept your client's goal of experiencing positive feelings about a negative A. It is unrealistic for your client to feel happy, for example, when he is faced with a negative life event that he would prefer not to encounter — for example, a loss or a failure, and so on. If you accept your client's goals of feeling positive about a negative event, you will encourage him to believe that it is good that the negative A occurred. Again, by doing this you will discourage him from thinking rationally. To reiterate a point that was made earlier, when you encourage your client to experience appropriate negative feelings in the face of negative life events, you help him: (a) to adjust positively to negative A; (b) to cope better with that A; and (c) to change A in more constructive ways.

Finally, do not accept vague goals — for example, 'I want to be happy.' The more specific you can encourage your client to be in setting goals, the more he will be motivated to do the hard work of changing his irrational beliefs in the service of achieving these goals.

Agree on Goals: Steve

I now knew that Steve was anxious about the threat of failure. My next task was to encourage him to feel concerned about the prospect of failure rather than anxious about it. However, this proved to be difficult, but I finally got through to Steve on this point in the following way.

> *Steve*: But if I'm concerned about the possibility of failure I'm admitting that it is a possibility. But I don't want to admit that.
>
> *Windy*: Because?
>
> *Steve*: Well, I believe that if you admit the possibility of failure you increase the chances that you may fail.
>
> *Windy*: Whereas if you tell yourself that failure won't happen?
>
> *Steve*: Then it won't.
>
> *Windy*: But if that was the case you wouldn't be here because all you would have to do would be to tell yourself that you wouldn't fail and that would guarantee that it wouldn't happen.
>
> *Steve*: I see what you mean.
>
> *Windy*: Now I've done some research to show that when you're anxious about something like failure you increase in your mind the chances that you might fail. However, when you're concerned but not anxious about failure you might admit the possibility that failure could happen but your feelings of concern would help you to act in a way so that failure is less likely rather than more likely to happen. So can you see that refusing to admit that failure is a possibility won't

help you? In fact it hasn't helped you. Also anxiety won't help you, we've seen that. But concern will help you because it will motivate you to work.

Steve: That's a novel way of looking at things.

Windy: Well, I'm pleased, but let's see if I've made myself clear. Can you put into your own words the point that I've been trying to make.

Steve: Concern helps you but anxiety doesn't. And thinking that something won't happen won't guarantee that it won't happen.

Windy: Right. So can we agree that we had better look failure in the eye and help you to feel concerned but not anxious about it?

Steve: Yes. I can see that now.

Windy: Now remember that doing so will probably help you to overcome your procrastination as well.

Step 5: Determine whether or not your Client has a Secondary Emotional Problem (and Assess if Appropriate)

Clients frequently have secondary emotional problems about their primary emotional problems and it is important to assess whether or not your client has such a secondary problem. If your client's primary problem is anxiety you may ask: 'How do you feel about feeling anxious?', to determine whether or not he does have a secondary emotional problem about his primary problem of anxiety.

When to Work on the Secondary Emotional Problem First
If your client does in fact have a secondary emotional problem, I suggest that you work on this problem first, under three conditions:

1 if the existence of your client's secondary problem interferes significantly (either in the session or in the client's life outside) with the work that you are trying to do with him on his primary problem;
2 if the secondary problem is more important of the two from a clinical perspective;
3 if your client can see the sense of working on his secondary emotional problem first. Here you may need to present a plausible rationale to your client for starting with his secondary problem first.

If your client still wishes to work on his primary problem first, after you have presented your rationale for starting with his secondary problem, then do so. To do otherwise may threaten the productive therapeutic alliance that you have by now established with your client.

Check for the Existence of an Emotional Problem about an Appropriate Negative Emotion
When you have assessed your client's *stated* primary problem you

may decide that he is, in fact, experiencing an appropriate negative emotion — for example, sadness in response to an important loss. If so, check whether your client has an emotional problem about this appropriate emotion. Your client may, for example, feel ashamed about feeling sad. If this is the case, define and agree that the secondary emotional problem (that is, shame) will be the client's target problem and proceed to carry out an ABC assessment of this agreed problem.

Assess the Presence of Shame if your Client is Reluctant to Disclose a Problem

As I noted earlier in this second part of the book, if your client is reluctant to disclose that he has an emotional problem, he may feel ashamed about either having the problem or disclosing it to you as a counsellor. When you suspect that this might be the case, ask your client how he would feel if he did have an emotional problem about the activating event that you are discussing. If he says that he would feel ashamed, agree with your client to work on shame as his target problem before encouraging him to disclose the original problem he had in mind.

Step 5: Steve
Steve did not have a secondary emotional problem about his anxiety or his procrastination.

Step 6: Teach the B–C Connection

By now you will have assessed the A and C elements of your client's primary or secondary problem. The next step is to teach your client that his emotional problem is largely determined by his beliefs rather than by the activating event that you have already assessed. Carrying out this step is important. Unless your client understands that his emotional problem is determined by his beliefs, then he will not understand why you are about to assess his beliefs in the next step of the treatment process. Spend some time, therefore, on teaching the B–C connection if he has difficulty in understanding it. The reader can consult several of the standard RET texts for exercises and metaphors to help teach this idea (Dryden, 1987c; Ellis and Dryden, 1987; Walen et al., 1980).

Step 6: Steve
Windy: Now since you can have different feelings about failure as we've agreed, can you see that it's not the prospect of failure that creates your feelings?

Steve: Yes.

Windy: Now the question is if an event doesn't lead to feelings, what does?

Steve: Well, Mike my friend who suggested that I come to see you told me that you both spent a lot of time looking at his attitudes. So I guess it's my attitudes that lead to my feelings.

Windy: That's right. As a famous philosopher, Epictetus, once said 'People are disturbed not by things but by the views they have of things.' Now let's see how this principle can be specifically applied to your anxiety about failing your PhD.

Step 7: Assess iB

Distinguish between Rational Beliefs and Irrational Beliefs
While assessing B keep clear in your mind the distinction between your client's rational beliefs (rB) and his irrational beliefs (iB) and help him to understand this distinction (see Part 1).

Assess both the Premiss Form of your Client's Irrational Belief and its Derivatives
In Part 1 of the book, I argued that your client's beliefs can be divided into a premiss and certain derivatives from this premiss. At this stage of the process you should be looking in particular to assess your client's *irrational* beliefs. As you do so, assess both the premiss form of the belief (for example, dogmatic musts, absolute shoulds, have to's, oughts, and so on) and the four main derivatives from the premiss (awfulising, I-can't-stand-it-itis, damnation, and always and never thinking). As you do this you can either teach and use the RET terms for these processes or you can use your client's own language, ensuring that his terms do accurately reflect irrational beliefs. Your choice here will be guided by your client's decision concerning which of these two strategies is the most helpful to him.

Remember the Three Basic Musts
While assessing your client's irrational beliefs keep in mind the three basic musts outlined in Part 1 — that is, demands about self, demands about others, and demands concerning the world and life conditions.

Distinguish between Absolute 'Shoulds' and other 'Shoulds'
While you are assessing the premiss form of your client's irrational beliefs, he may use the word 'should', which has several different meanings in the English language. Rational-emotive theory hypothesises that only *absolute* 'shoulds' are related to emotional distur-

bance; other meanings of the word 'should' do not account for your client's emotional problems — such as 'shoulds' of preference; empirical 'shoulds' — that is, when two parts of hydrogen and one part of oxygen are mixed you *should* get water; and 'shoulds' of recommendation — for example, you *should* go and see that excellent play at the local theatre. In particular, help your client to distinguish between his absolute 'shoulds' and his 'shoulds' of preference. If your client finds the different meanings of the word 'should' confusing, it may be helpful to use the word 'must' instead, when referring to the possible existence of an irrational belief in its premiss form. It is Albert Ellis's and my clinical experience that the word 'must' better conveys the meaning of absolutistic demandingness than the word 'should'.

Using Questions in Assessing iB
When you assess your client's irrational beliefs, use questions. A standard question that rational-emotive counsellors frequently use is: 'What were you telling yourself about A to make yourself disturbed at C?'. This type of question has both advantages and disadvantages. The advantage is that it is open-ended and in using it you will be unlikely to put words into your client's mouth concerning the content of his belief. On the other hand, bear in mind that your client will most likely respond by not articulating an irrational belief. Rather, he is most likely to give you further inferences about A and ones that may well be less relevant than the one you selected at step 4. Thus, for example, imagine your client is anxious in particular about other people thinking him a fool if he stammers in public. Asking him the question 'What were you telling yourself about others thinking of you as a fool to make yourself anxious?' might yield the response 'I thought they wouldn't like me.' Note that this thought is another inference and you still do not know what your client's irrational belief is. In this instance, help the client to understand that this is not an irrational belief but a further inference and educate him to look for his irrational belief about A. You can do this by the judicious use of open-ended questions combined with some didactic explanation.

What other kinds of open-ended questions can you use when assessing your client's irrational beliefs? Walen et al. (1980) list a number, including: 'What was going through your mind?'; 'Were you aware of any thoughts in your head?'; 'What was on your mind then?; 'Are you aware of what you were thinking at that moment?', and so on. Again, note that your client may not spontaneously disclose irrational beliefs in response to these questions, and will need additional didactic help in this regard.

An alternative to asking open-ended questions at A is asking theory-driven questions — that is, questions that are directly derived from rational-emotive theory. Thus, for example, instead of asking your client, 'What were you telling yourself about the other people's criticism to make yourself disturbed at C?', you might ask him, 'What *demand* were you making about other people's criticism to make yourself disturbed at point C?'. The advantage here is that a theory-driven question orients your client to look for his irrational beliefs. The danger is that you may be putting words into your client's mouth and in fact encourage him to look for irrational beliefs that he may not have. However, if you have established that your client has a negative inappropriate emotion at point C you will minimise this danger.

I have already provided an example of a theory-driven question about a must (premiss). An example of one designed to assess the presence of a derivative from a must is: 'What kind of person did you think you were for stammering and incurring other people's criticism?'

Step 7: Steve

Windy: Right, so to recap, you're anxious about failing your PhD. Now we've agreed that it's not failing that makes you anxious but your attitude about it. Now it's important to distinguish between two types of attitude, one that will lead to anxiety and other self-defeating emotions, while the other will lead to concern and other constructive emotions. So if you bear with me, before we focus directly on your anxiety, I want to take you through an example that will help you to understand this important distinction, OK?

Steve: OK.

Windy: Now, I want you to imagine that you have £10 in your pocket and that your attitude is that you prefer to have a minimum of £11 at all times, but that it's not essential. How will you feel about having £10 while you want to have £11?

Steve: Concerned?

Windy: Right, or frustrated, but you wouldn't want to commit suicide. Right?

Steve: That's right.

Windy: Now this time imagine that your attitude is 'I absolutely must have a minimum of £11 at all times, I must, I must, I must', and you look in your pocket and discover that you only have £10. Now how will you feel?

Steve: Anxious.

Windy: Or depressed. Note that it's the same situation, but a different attitude or belief. Now the third scenario. Again you have that same dogmatic belief 'I must have a minimum of £11 at all times, I must, I must, I must.' But now you look in your pocket and you find that you've got £12. Now how will you feel?

Steve: Pleased.

Windy: That's right, or relieved. But with that same belief, 'I must have a minimum of £11 at all times', you would soon have a thought that will lead you to make yourself anxious again. What do you think that thought would be?

Steve: That I might lose £2?

Windy: Right, I might lose £2, or I might spend it or get robbed. Now the point of this is that all humans, black or white, rich or poor, male or female, will make themselves emotionally disturbed if they don't get what they believe they *must* get. And they will also make themselves disturbed when they do, because of their *demands*, their *musts*. Because even if they have what they think they *must* have, they could always lose it. But when humans stick to their non-dogmatic desires and don't escalate these into dogmatic musts they will constructively adjust when they don't get what they want or be able to take effective action to try to prevent something undesirable happening in the future. Now I want you to keep in mind this distinction between non-dogmatic wants and absolute musts as we go back to your own situation. OK?

Steve: Fine.

Windy: Now, what do you think your demand is about failing that leads to your anxiety?

Steve: I must not fail.

Windy: Right and what kind of person do you think you would be in your own mind if you do fail?

Steve: A failure.

In this case I chose to teach Steve the RET model of emotional disturbance by using an example unrelated to his own problem before assessing his irrational beliefs. I considered that as Steve could deal effectively with abstract concepts and seemed to learn quickly that this would be a particularly effective method for both assessing his irrational beliefs and for teaching him the ABCs of RET.

Step 8: Connect iB and C

After you have accurately assessed your client's irrational beliefs, in the form of both a premiss and its derivatives, ensure that your client understands the connection between his irrational beliefs (iB) and his disturbed emotions at point C before proceeding to dispute these beliefs. Thus, you might say, 'Can you understand that as long as you demand that other people must not criticise you, you are bound to make yourself anxious about this happening?' or 'Can you see that as long as you believe that you are no good for being regarded by others as a fool, you will be anxious about being criticised?' If your client says 'yes', then you can ask 'So, in order to change your feeling of anxiety to one of concern, what do you need to change first?' If your client says that he understands that he had better change his belief in order to change his feeling, eliciting the iB–C connection is likely to be more productive than telling your client that this is the case. Telling your client about the iB–C connection does not mean that he will understand it. If your client does not see the connection between his irrational belief and C, spend time helping him to understand it before beginning to dispute his irrational beliefs.

Step 8: Steve

> *Windy*: So can you see that as long as you believe that you must not fail and that you would be a failure if you did, that you will be anxious and thus tend to procrastinate?
>
> *Steve*: Yes, that's clear.
>
> *Windy*: So in order to change your anxiety to feelings of concern and thus to stop procrastinating what do you need to change first?
>
> *Steve*: The beliefs that I must not fail and that I'm a failure if I do fail.

Step 9: Dispute iB

The Goals of Disputing

The major goal of disputing at this stage of the RET treatment process is to encourage your client to understand that his irrational beliefs are unproductive (that is, they lead to self-defeating emotions), illogical, and inconsistent with reality, and that the rational alternative to these beliefs (that is, his rational beliefs) are productive, logical, and consistent with reality. If you succeed in helping your client to achieve such understanding, do not, however, expect that his conviction in the rational belief will be strong at this stage. Help your client to distinguish between light conviction and deep conviction in a rational belief. Also encourage him to see that at this stage even a light conviction in the rational alternative belief (also known as intellectual understanding) is a sign of progress, albeit insufficient in itself to promote emotional change.

More specifically with respect to the target problem, the goals of disputing are to help your client to understand the following:

1 *Musts*: that there is no evidence in support of his absolute demand while evidence does exist for his preference. As Albert Ellis often says, 'There are most likely no absolute musts in the universe.';

2 *Awfulising*: that what he has defined as 'awful' (that is, 101 per cent bad) is magical nonsense, and that in reality it will lie within a 0–99.999 per cent scale of badness;

3   *I-can't-stand-it-itis*: that your client can virtually always stand
    what he thinks he can't stand, and that he can find some
    happiness, even if bad events at A continue;
4   *Damnation*: that this is a concept which is inconsistent with
    reality, is illogical, and will lead your client into emotional
    trouble, and that the alternative is for him to accept himself,
    other people, and the world as fallible and complex — too
    complex to be given a single global rating;
5   *Always and never thinking*: that it is most unlikely that the client,
    for example, will always be rejected and never succeed in doing
    well. He is not intrinsically *unlovable*, nor a total *failure*.

Much later on in the treatment process your goal is to help your
client internalise a broad range of rational beliefs, so that they
become part of a general philosophy of rational living (but this is
beyond the scope of this part of the book).

Using Questions during Disputing

Let us assume that you are now going to dispute your client's
irrational belief in the form of a must. The first stage in the
disputing sequence is to ask for evidence in support of the must.
Standard questions of this type are: 'Where is the evidence that you
must under all conditions succeed?'; 'Where is the proof?'; 'Is it
true . . .?'; 'Can you prove that you must . . .?'; 'Where is it written
that you must . . .?', and so on.

Ensure that your client answers the actual question that you have
asked. He may well answer a question that he thinks you have
asked. Thus, for example, in response to the question 'Why must
you succeed?', your client might say, 'Because it would bring me
advantages if I succeed.' Note that your client has not addressed
himself to the actual question that you have asked, but to a different
question, namely; 'Why is it preferable for you to succeed?'
Another way to consider this interchange would be that your client
has answered your question, but incorrectly. Remember that according to RET theory, the only correct answer to the question,
'Why must you succeed?' is 'There is no reason why I must succeed.'
Thus, if your client gives any other answer, you know that he is
wrong, or is providing an answer to a different question. In fact,
anticipate that your client will not quickly provide a correct answer
to your question, 'Why must you succeed?' Assuming that your
client has not answered your actual question correctly, you need to
educate him concerning why his answers are either: (a) incorrect
with respect to the question that you *have* asked; or (b) correct
responses to a different question. During this process use a combi-

nation of questions and short didactic explanations, until your client gives the correct answer (for example, 'There is no evidence why I must succeed, but I would prefer to.') and understands why it is correct.

As a part of this process, again help your client to distinguish between his irrational beliefs and his rational beliefs. A good example of doing this is as follows. Write two questions on a board — for example, 'Why must you succeed?', and 'Why is it preferable but not essential for you to succeed?' Ask your client to answer both questions. Note that he may well give you the same answers to the two different questions. If so, help your client to see that the reasons he has given constitute evidence for his rational belief, but not his irrational belief. As I have already stressed, help him to see that the only answer to a question about the existence of musts is 'There are probably no absolute musts in the universe.'

Be Persistent and do not Switch

I argued earlier that it is important for you to dispute your client's irrational beliefs, in the form of both a premiss (must) and at least one of the four derivatives from that premiss (awfulising, I-can't-stand-it-itis, damnation, and always and never thinking). However, do not switch from disputing one to disputing the other until you are finished, as this will be very confusing for your client. If you have decided to dispute the irrational premiss, persist with this until you have successfully shown your client that there is no evidence in support of his must before switching to disputing a derivative from that premiss. However, if you have persisted in disputing an irrational premiss and it is clear that your client is not finding this helpful, then switch to disputing a derivative and monitor your client's reactions. Some clients find it easier to understand why these irrational derivatives are irrational than why their musts are irrational.

Use a Variety of Disputing Strategies

There are three basic disputing strategies, and it is best to use all three if you can.

Strategy 1: Focus on Illogicality   Your purpose here is to help your client to understand why his irrational belief is illogical. In doing so, ask the question; 'Where is the logic?' rather than 'Where is the evidence?' Help your client to understand that because he wants something to happen it is not logical for him to believe that therefore it absolutely must happen. Stress to your client that his must about his preference is magical and does not follow logically from the preference.

Strategy 2: Focus on Empiricism   Your goal here is to show your client that his musts and associated derivatives from these musts are almost always empirically inconsistent with reality. As such, use questions which ask your client to provide evidence in support of his irrational beliefs: for example, 'Where is the evidence . . .?' Help your client to understand that if there was evidence in support of his belief 'I must succeed', then he would have to succeed, no matter what he believed. If he is not succeeding at present, that fact constitutes evidence that his irrational belief 'I must succeed' is empirically inconsistent with reality.

Strategy 3: Focus on Pragmatism   The purpose of focusing on the pragmatic consequences of your client holding irrational beliefs is to show him that as long as he believes in his irrational musts and their derivatives, he is going to remain disturbed. Thus, ask such questions as: 'Where is believing that you must succeed going to get you other than anxious and depressed?'

Once the irrational belief has been disputed, it is important that your client learns to replace it with a new rational belief. Work together with your client to construct a rational belief which is most adaptive with respect to A. After you have helped your client to construct an alternative rational belief, dispute it logically, empirically, and pragmatically. Do this to help your client see that rational beliefs are in fact rational. It is much better for your client to hold rational beliefs because he has seen for himself that there is evidence for them than because you have told them that they are rational.

Use a Variety of Disputing Styles
At this early stage of your career as a rational-emotive counsellor I suggest that you use four basic styles of disputing your client's irrational beliefs.

The Socratic Style   When you use the Socratic style of disputing, your main task is to ask questions concerning the illogical, empirically inconsistent, and dysfunctional aspects of your client's irrational beliefs, although these questions may be interspersed with brief explanations which are designed to correct your client's misconceptions of these points. The purpose of Socratic disputing is to encourage your client to think for himself, rather than to accept your viewpoint just because you have some authority as a therapist.

The Didactic Style   While rational-emotive counsellors prefer using Socratic-type disputing, this does not always prove productive and you may have to shift to giving lengthy didactic explanations concerning why an irrational belief is self-defeating and why a rational belief is more productive. Indeed, you will probably have to use didactic explanations with all your clients at some point in the treatment process, although with some you will need to use this method more extensively than with others. When you use lengthy didactic explanations with your client, ensure that he understands what you have been saying. After you have given a didactic explanation ask your client to explain in his own words his understanding of the point you have tried to make. Thus, for example, ask: 'I'm not quite sure whether I'm making myself clear here, perhaps you could put into our own words what you think I've been saying to you?' Do not necessarily accept your client's non-verbal and para-verbal signs of understanding (for example, head nods and hmm hmm's) as evidence that he has in fact understood you. Remember the maxim: 'There is no good course without a test!'

Humour With some clients a productive way of making the point that there is no evidence for their irrational beliefs is to use humour or humorous exaggeration. An example is provided by Walen et al. (1980: 101):

> . . . if the client says, "It's really awful that I failed the test!", the therapist might respond, "You're right! It's not only awful, but I don't see how you're going to survive. That's the worst news I've ever heard. This is so horrendous that I can't bear to talk about it. Let's talk about something else quick!". Such paradoxical statements frequently point out the senselessness of the irrational belief to the client and very little further debate may be necessary to make the point.

However, your use of humorous exaggeration as a disputing strategy does depend upon a number of factors: first, that you have established a good relationship with your client; secondly, that he has already shown some evidence that he has a sense of humour; and thirdly, that your humorous intervention is *directed* at the *irrationality* of the client's irrational belief and *not* at the *client* as a person.

Therapist Self-disclosure Another constructive way of disputing your client's irrational beliefs is for you to use self-disclosure. Here you would disclose (a) that you have experienced a problem similar to that of your client; (b) that you once believed in an irrational belief similar to your client's but no longer do so; and (c) how you changed this belief. This is known as the 'coping model' of self-disclosure. Thus, for example, I have used the personal example of how I overcame my anxiety about stammering in public, and thus stammered less. What I do is to disclose that I used to believe: 'I must not stammer.' I stress that this belief increased rather than diminished my anxiety. I then show how I disputed this irrational belief by proving to myself that there was no evidence to support this belief and changed it to a rational belief: 'There's no reason why I must not stammer. If I stammer, I stammer, that's unfortunate, but hardly awful.' I then describe how I then pushed myself to put this rational belief into practice while speaking in public and finally outline the productive effects that I experienced through doing so. This 'coping model' contrasts with a 'mastery model' of self-disclosure. In the latter you disclose the fact that you have never experienced a similar problem to that of your client, because you have always thought rationally about the issue at hand. The 'mastery model' tends to accentuate the differences between you and your client and in my experience is less productive than the 'coping model' in encouraging your client to challenge his own irrational belief. So whenever possible, and appropriate, use a 'coping model' of self-disclosure. However, some of your clients will not find even the 'coping model' useful, and if this is the case, avoid using self-disclosure as a disputing strategy with such clients.

Be Creative while Disputing

The more experience you gain disputing irrational beliefs, the more you will develop your own individual style of disputing. Thus, you will build up a repertoire of various stories, aphorisms, metaphors, and other examples to show your clients why their irrational beliefs are indeed irrational, and why their rational alternative will promote psychological health. I will now give some examples of creative disputing.

In working with clients who believe that they must not experience panic and could not stand it if they did, I use what I call 'The Shi'ite dispute'. I ask: 'Let's suppose that your parents have been captured by the Shi'ite Muslims and they will only release your parents if you agree to put up with ten panic attacks. Will you do so?' The client invariably says: 'Yes'. If so, I will then say: 'But I thought you couldn't stand the experience of panic?' The client usually replies, 'Well, but I would do it in order to save my parents.' To this I reply: 'Yes, but will you do it for your own mental health?'

Another creative disputing strategy is what I call 'The friend dispute'. Imagine that your client has failed at an important test and believes: 'I must do well and I am no good if I don't.' Ask him whether he would condemn his best friend for a similar failure in the same way as he condemns himself. Normally your client will say 'No.' If so, point out to him that he has a different attitude to his friend than he has towards himself. Suggest that if he chose to be as compassionate towards himself as he is towards his friend, he would help himself to solve his own emotional problems.

I end this section on disputing with one piece of advice: Master the basics of disputing before trying to be too creative.

Step 9: Steve

Windy: OK, so let's take those beliefs 'I must not fail my PhD' and 'I would be a failure if I fail my PhD' one at a time. They're really linked but it's better if we look at them separately. OK?

Steve: Fine.

Windy: Now I'm going to help you to re-evaluate those two beliefs. Let's take the first one. There are basically three ways of challenging this belief. First to ask whether or not it is logical; secondly to check whether or not it is consistent with reality; and thirdly to consider its effects. First let's look at the logical argument. Now remember you don't want to fail your PhD. Right?

Steve: Right.

Windy: But is it good logic to conclude that because you do not want to fail your PhD therefore you must not fail it?

Steve: Do you mean does it follow logically?

Windy: Right, that's a better way of putting it.

Steve: No, it doesn't follow.

Windy: Why not?

Steve: [*Pause*] . . . Well, I guess just because I don't want something to happen doesn't mean that it logically follows that it must not happen.

Windy: That's right. To demand that something must not happen simply because you don't want it to happen is really to believe in magic. If magic did exist then all you'd have to do is to want something and it would have to be yours. Now does magic exist?

Steve: No, of course not. I've always thought that a belief in magic was illogical so I can see what you mean.

Windy: Right, so let's move on to see whether your belief 'I must not fail my PhD' is consistent with reality. If there was such a law of the universe then what would have to follow?

Steve: I'm not sure what you're getting at.

Windy: OK. Let me give you an example. Given the conditions that exist in the world at present there is a law of the universe which states that if you take two parts of hydrogen and add it to one part of oxygen you *must* get what?

Steve: Water.

Windy: Right. It's not an absolute law for all time because atmospheric and other conditions might change and who knows what you'll get then. But at present the law, 'Add two parts of hydrogen to one part of oxygen and you must get water' is consistent with reality. Right?

Steve: Right.

Windy: Now, if the law 'I must not fail my PhD' were consistent with reality, how could you possibly fail?

Steve: I couldn't.

Windy: Why not?

Steve: Well, I would have to go along with the law whether I wanted to or not.

Windy: That's a very important point. You would have no choice but to pass your PhD. But obviously you have a choice. You could give it up and climb a mountain or do a thousand other things. So there is no law of the universe which decrees that you must not fail your PhD. You've invented it and as such you could repeal the law and stick to your preference.

Steve: You mean the belief 'I don't want to fail my PhD'?

Windy: Or to express it in full 'I don't want to fail my PhD but there's no reason why I must not fail it.'

Steve: Oh, right, that last bit is important.

Windy: Right. You see if you just say 'I don't want to fail my PhD' being human you could always sneak in . . . 'and therefore I must not fail it'. However, if you express it in full there's less of a danger of sneaking in that 'must'.

Steve: Yes, I can see that.

Windy: Now, is that belief 'I don't want to fail my PhD but there's no reason why I must not fail it' consistent with reality?

Steve: Well, it's consistent with the reality of my preference.

Windy: That's right. The reality is that you have that preference. Good. Now let's have a look at the usefulness of the belief, which is the third way of challenging it. Now as long as you believe that 'you must not fail your PhD' what are going to be the consequences of holding that belief?

Steve: That I'm going to become anxious.

Windy: And procrastinate.

Steve: Correct.

Windy: So the belief is going to get you into trouble, emotionally and behaviourally. Now what will be the consequences of your non-absolute preference 'I don't want to fail my PhD but there's no reason why I must not fail it'?

Steve: Well, as we said earlier I'd feel concerned and that concern would motivate me to study.

Windy: That's the point. Good. So the three ways of challenging an absolute must involve asking, first, Is it logical?; secondly, Is it consistent with reality?; and thirdly, Will it give me good results? Now as we've seen on the whole the answer to all these questions is 'no'. But don't take my word for it, think it through for yourself. Incidentally, as we've done you can also use these three questions with your non-absolute preferences.

Steve: Right, let me make a note of that.

Windy: It's on tape.[5]

Steve: Yes, but I want to get it down while it's fresh in my mind . . . [*pause*] . . .

Windy: Fine. Now let's use the same three questions with your second belief, 'I would be a failure if I failed my PhD'. First, is it logical to conclude that you would be a failure if you failed in one area of your life?

Steve: Well, it's a very important area of my life.

Windy: Agreed, but if I've understood you right you would condemn your whole self for one failure, is that right?

Steve: Right.

Windy: So, no matter how important succeeding is to you, is it logical to conclude that your whole self is a failure just because you have failed, albeit in a very important part of your life?

Steve: No, I suppose not.

Windy: You don't sound too sure.

Steve: No, I was just thinking that I've always believed that I would be a failure if I failed at something really important.

Windy: Right, but that's what human beings tend to do. We don't usually conclude 'I'm a failure' if we fail at something unimportant like tiddlywinks unless we're really crazy. But most of us will have a tendency to put ourselves down when we fail at something when we would strongly prefer to be successful. That's because we also sneak in a must. But it's illogical to put ourselves down because in doing so we jump from rating a part of ourselves as negative to rating our whole selves as negative. It's the part — whole leap that's illogical.

Steve: Yes, I can see that.

Windy: In fact we would do better not to rate our 'selves' at all. Do you know why?

Steve: No, why?

Windy: Well let me see if I can help you see why. Now try and give this room a single rating that completely accounts for it.

Steve: It's a comfortable room.

Windy: No, you're rating a dimension of the room — the dimension of comfort. But I asked you to rate the room in a way that completely accounts for it.

Steve: You can't.

Windy: That's right. But why is that the right answer?

Steve: Because it's too complex to be summed up in one rating.

Windy: Now, what's more complex, you or the room?

Steve: Oh, I get it. I'm too complex to be given a single rating . . . [*pause*] . . . I like that idea.

Windy: Right and when you say 'I'm a failure', you are denying that complexity. Now if you were a single-cell amoeba and that single cell was a failure, perhaps you could legitimately conclude 'I'm a failure.' But are you a single-cell amoeba?

Steve: [*Laughs*] Of course not.

Windy: But it makes sense to rate aspects of yourself, since that's how we can improve our performance. But the important point here is that you accept yourself as a fallible human being — too complex to be given a single rating.

Now, let's move on to the second point. If the belief 'I am a failure' were consistent with reality, what would you only be able to do in life?

Steve: Fail.

Windy: That's right. Now is that what you only do in life?

Steve: No, of course not. In fact I've rarely failed at important things.

Windy: Right. Now, let's consider the alternative belief 'If I fail at my

PhD that proves I'm a fallible human being, too complex to be given a single rating.' Is that consistent with reality?

Steve: Yes it is.

Windy: Now the third point. As long as you believe you would be a failure if you failed your PhD where will that belief get you?

Steve: The same place as the must — anxious and procrastinating.

Windy: And the alternative belief?

Steve: You mean I'm too complex to be given a single rating?

Windy: And fallible.

Steve: Again concerned because I still wouldn't want to fail.

Windy: Good. So again to recap you can use the logical argument, the consistent-with-reality argument and the pragmatic argument on both your musts and self-downing beliefs etc., and on your preferences and self-acceptance beliefs. But the important point is for you to think it through for yourself. Ask yourself similar questions as I've been asking you, and think through the answers.

Step 10: Prepare your Client to Deepen his Conviction in his Rational Beliefs

Once your client has acknowledged that (a) there no evidence in support of his irrational beliefs but there is evidence to support his rational beliefs; (b) it would be more logical for him to think rationally; and (c) his rational beliefs will lead him to more productive emotional results than his irrational beliefs, you are in a position to begin to help him to deepen his conviction in his rational beliefs.

Point out why a Weak Conviction in Rational Beliefs is Insufficient to Promote Change

Start by helping your client to understand why a weak conviction in rational beliefs, while important, is insufficient to promote change. Do this by discussing briefly the rational-emotive view of therapeutic change. Using Socratic questioning and brief didactic explanations, help your client to see that he will strengthen his conviction in his rational beliefs by disputing his irrational beliefs and replacing them with their rational alternatives within and between therapy sessions. Also help your client to understand that this process requires him to act against his irrational beliefs as well as to dispute them cognitively. Establishing this now will help you later when you reach the stages of encouraging your client to put his new learning into practice (step 11) and of facilitating the working-through process (step 13).

Deal with the 'Head–Gut' Issue

As you help your client to think rationally he may say something like: 'I understand my rational belief will help me to achieve my goals but I don't really believe in it yet', or 'I understand it intellectually but not emotionally', or 'I understand it in my head but not in my gut.' Indeed, you may wish to anticipate this issue by bringing it up yourself as a prelude to discussing with your client how he is going to deepen his conviction in his rational belief and weaken his conviction in his irrational belief. You might ask, for example: 'What do you think you will have to do in order to get your new rational belief into your gut?'

Help your client to commit himself to a process of therapeutic change which requires him to dispute his irrational beliefs repeatedly and forcefully and to practise thinking rationally in relevant life contexts. As you will see below this process involves him using a variety of homework assignments.

Step 10: Steve

Windy: Now, how often do you think you will have to question and change your self-defeating beliefs before you begin to believe the alternative constructive beliefs?

Steve: Quite often, I suppose.

Windy: Why should that be so?

Steve: I guess because I've held my self-defeating beliefs for quite a while.

Windy: That's right. Imagine that when you were young you wanted to play golf and an uncle said he would teach you. Unfortunately he taught you incorrectly but as you were keen, you practised these incorrect strokes diligently not knowing, of course, that they were wrong. However, your golf handicap kept increasing. Now imagine that later you realised what had happened and you went to have lessons from a golf pro. He was able to diagnose the problem and showed you how to play the strokes correctly. Now what would you need to do in order to improve your golfing play?

Steve: Keep practising the new strokes.

Windy: That's right, but what would happen at the beginning?

Steve: I'm not sure what you mean.

Windy: Well, would you be comfortable playing the new strokes?

Steve: No.

Windy: Why not?

Steve: Because my habit would be to play the stroke incorrectly. That would be my natural feeling.

Windy: Right, but would having that natural feeling stop you from correcting the stroke when you realised that it was incorrect?

Steve: No, it wouldn't.

Windy: Right. Now it's the same with belief change. The next time you think about working it's quite likely that you will believe 'I must not fail my PhD and I would be a failure if I did fail.' It's likely because that's what you've believed in the past and it's fairly natural to you. But if you don't go along with that natural feeling you can identify, challenge, and change these beliefs and keep doing so until the new way of thinking comes more naturally to you. Also the more you act according to the new belief the more you will enhance this process. Is that clear?

Steve: Yes, I need to challenge and change my self-defeating beliefs frequently and act as if I believed the new belief.

Windy: Right, until the new belief which you now believe lightly becomes a part of you. It's what some of my clients call going from 'head belief' to 'gut belief'. What they mean by this is that there is a process from seeing lightly that the rational belief is true to really believing that it is true in your gut. Now that takes a lot of practice.

Step 11: Homework: Encourage your Client to Put his New Learning into Practice

Your client is now ready to put into practice his rational belief. Remind your client again about the rational-emotive theory of change: that in order to deepen his conviction in his rational belief, he needs to practise disputing his irrational beliefs and strengthen his rational beliefs in situations which are the same or similar to the activating event that has already been assessed. Help your client to choose from a wide variety of homework assignments, that are advocated in RET. These include behavioural assignments, emotive-evocative assignments, cognitive assignments (where your client disputes his irrational beliefs either in written form or in his mind), and imagery assignments (see Part 3 for further information about these techniques).

Ensure that the Homework Assignment is Relevant to Changing the Target Irrational Belief
Make sure that homework assignments are relevant to changing the irrational belief that has been targeted for change and that if the client carries out these asssignments, doing so will help him to deepen his conviction in the rational alternative — that is, his rational belief.

Collaborate with your Client
While you are discussing appropriate homework assignments with your client enlist his active collaboration in the process. Ensure that he can see the sense of carrying out the homework assignment; that if he does it, it will help him to achieve his goals; and that he has some degree of confidence that he can in fact carry out the assignment. Maximise the chances that your client will do the assignment by helping him to specify *when* he might do it, in *which* context, and *how frequently*.

Encourage your Client to Carry out an 'Ideal' Homework
Assignment but be Prepared to Compromise
An 'ideal' homework assignment will involve the client actively disputing his irrational beliefs in a forceful manner and in the most relevant context. Try, if you can, to encourage your client to carry out an 'ideal' assignment. If this is not possible then encourage him, first, to dispute his irrational beliefs in situations which approximate the most relevant A or secondly, to use imagery and dispute his irrational beliefs while vividly imagining A. You may find that if your client does these less 'ideal' assignments then he may be more likely to carry out the 'ideal' assignment later.

Assess and Trouble-shoot Obstacles to Completion of
Homework Assignments
While you are negotiating appropriate homework assignments with your client encourage him to specify any obstacles that might serve to prevent him from doing the assignment once he has agreed to do it. Encourage your client, if possible, to find ways of overcoming those obstacles in advance of carrying out the assignment.

General Comments about Homework Assignments
For the purposes of clarity I have focused on homework assignments which involve your client strengthening his conviction in his rational beliefs. However, you can employ homework assignments at any point during the rational-emotive treatment sequence. Thus, you might encourage your client to carry out a homework assignment which may help him to: (a) specify his troublesome emotions at C; (b) detect his irrational beliefs at B; and (c) identify the most relevant aspect of A about which he has made himself particularly disturbed.

You may also employ homework assignments as part of the process where you educate your client concerning the 'ABC's of RET'. Here you might ask your client to read various RET books (bibliotherapy) or to listen to RET lectures on audio tape. When doing so, choose material that is relevant to your client's problem and which the client can readily understand. In special circumstances you may even make a tape which is tailor-made for your client's particular problem where there is no appropriate material readily available.

Rational-emotive counsellors suggest that their clients use a variety of assignments and these will be discussed in greater detail in Part 3. However, these can be divided into four major categories. First, there are a number of *cognitive assignments* that you can suggest to your client to encourage him to practise disputing his irrational beliefs. These vary in simplicity and structure (see, for example, Figure 3, p. 74–5).

Secondly, *imagery assignments* are also employed. These are particularly helpful when you wish to encourage your client to gain confidence that he can carry out the assignment *in vivo*. In addition, rational-emotive imagery (REI) (see Part 3; Maultsby and Ellis, 1974; Walen et al., 1980) enables your client to practise disputing his irrational beliefs. This is achieved when he deliberately changes his negative inappropriate emotion to a negative appropriate emotion, while all the time vividly imagining the troublesome activating event at A.

Thirdly, rational-emotive counsellors favour *behavioural assignments* which involve clients confronting straight away the troublesome situations about which they make themselves disturbed, while simultaneously disputing their irrational beliefs in these contexts. As noted earlier, your client may refuse to do this assignment (known as *in vivo* flooding). If so you can encourage your client to choose a particular assignment which he finds 'challenging but not overwhelming'. Try, however, to dissuade your client from carrying out an assignment which does not involve some level of discomfort for him. Whatever behavioural assignment you negotiate with your client, ensure that it is both legal and ethical.

Finally, emotive-evocative assignments are used in which clients bring force and energy to the three types of assignments mentioned above.

Step 11: Steve

    Windy: Since changing your beliefs takes a lot of practice I will suggest throughout counselling that you put into practice between sessions what you learn inside sessions. What do you think of that idea?

    Steve: It sounds fine. I'm keen to start putting things into practice.

    Windy: Good, so let's make a start. What do you think you can do between now and next week to strengthen the beliefs: 'I don't want to fail my PhD but there is no reason why I must not fail it' and 'If I fail my PhD I'm not a failure, I'm a fallible human being for having failed'?

    Steve: Well, I can go over the arguments that we went over.

    Windy: How frequently?

    Steve: Three times a day?

    Windy: Does that sound feasible?

    Steve: Yes, I can manage that.

    Windy: When will you do it?

    Steve: Morning, noon, and night, to quote a phrase.

    Windy: [*Laughs*] Right, but that phrase really means that you won't stop practising. So let's agree a time limit.

Steve: How about ten minutes in the morning, ten minutes in the afternoon, and ten minutes in the evening.
Windy: Sounds fine. Now can you see any obstacles to doing this?
Steve: Well since I've been procrastinating I might put off the practice.
Windy: How might you do this?
Steve: Oh, by telling myself I'll do it later.
Windy: How could you overcome this obstacle?
Steve: By postponing pleasurable activities until I've done it.
Windy: Will that work?
Steve: Yes, I believe that it will.

Step 12: Check Homework Assignments

Once you have negotiated a particular homework assignment with your client and he has undertaken to carry it out, check, at the beginning of the next session, on what he learned from the experience. If you fail to do this you show your client that you do not consider homework assignments to be an important ingredient of the process of change; whereas, in reality, such assignments play a central role in helping your client to achieve his therapeutic goals.

Check that your Client Really Faced A

Remember that homework assignments are designed to solve emotional problems, not practical problems. Clients are prone to develop strategies to avoid A's rather than strategies to confront A's and change C's. So when you check on your client's experience in carrying out the assignment, make sure that he actually faced A that he committed himself to confront. If your client has done this he will usually report that he first made himself disturbed and then used the homework assignment to make himself undisturbed in the same situation. If your client has not done this, point this out to him, deal with any obstacles involved, and encourage him once more to confront the situation and to use vigorous disputing to make himself undisturbed in that context. If necessary, model appropriate disputes and encourage your client to rehearse these in the session and before facing the situation in question.

Check that your Client Actually Changed B

If your client reports a successful experience in carrying out the homework assignment, assess whether his success can be attributed to him (a) changing his irrational belief to its rational alternative; (b) changing either A itself or his inferences about A; or (c) using distraction techniques. If your client used the last two of these methods, acknowledge the client's efforts but point out that these methods may not be helpful to him in the long term. Stress that practical homework solutions or distractions are only palliative because one has not learned to change the inappropriate negative emotion which will then still exist to disturb the client if unavoidable A's are present. Once again encourage him to face the same situation at A but this time elicit his commitment that he will dispute his irrational beliefs and practise acting on the basis of his new rational beliefs.

When your Client Fails to Carry out the Homework Assignment

If your client has failed to execute the agreed homework assignment accept him as a fallible human being for his failure and help him to identify reasons why he did not carry out the assignment. In particular, use the ABC framework to encourage your client to focus on possible irrational beliefs that he held which served to prevent him from carrying out the homework assignment. Assess, in particular, whether or not your client held irrational beliefs indicating a philosophy of low frustration tolerance — for example: 'It was too hard'; 'I couldn't be bothered'; 'I shouldn't have to work hard in counselling', and so on. If your client has such beliefs, encourage him to challenge and change them and then reassign the homework assignment.

If you have difficulty clarifying reasons why your client did not carry out the homework assignment, you could ask him to fill out a form designed to identify possible reasons (see Appendix 1).

Step 12: Steve

Windy: How did you get on with your homework assignment, which was challenging your irrational beliefs three times a day?

Steve: Well, like the curate's egg. Good in parts.

Windy: What do you mean?

Steve: Well, I made a good start. I went over the tape of the session and made notes about how to challenge my self-defeating beliefs using the three arguments we discussed and I did what I agreed to do for the first two days. Then it tailed off.

Windy: What do you mean, 'tailed off'?

Steve: Well, let me see. I made a note of what I did and didn't do. On Monday and Tuesday, like I said — three times a day. No problem, and I was getting pretty good at it. On Wednesday I missed the morning, did it half-heartedly in the afternoon, and then nothing until yesterday, but that was out of guilt.

Windy: OK, first let's acknowledge that you did really well for the first two days. Now let's have a closer look at what happened on Wednesday. First, what did you tell yourself to miss the practice on Wednesday morning?

Steve: It's getting tedious.

Windy: But that wouldn't be enough to stop you from doing the practice.

Because you could then say first, 'OK so it's getting tedious. Tough, I'll do it anyway', and secondly, 'How can I make it less tedious?' So the observation that it was getting tedious didn't stop you. What did you tell yourself implicitly about the tedium to stop yourself from doing the practice?

Steve: Oh, I see, yeah, of course 'It must not be tedious.'

Windy: Right. Now how could you challenge that idea?

Steve: By proving to myself that there is no reason why it must not be tedious, that I would like it to be fascinating but it doesn't have to be and that I can do it even if it isn't fascinating.

Windy: Right, but can you throw yourself into it if it isn't fascinating or will you do it half-heartedly?

Steve: No, I can still do it thoroughly even if it isn't fascinating and as you implied earlier I can experiment to see if I can make it more interesting.

Windy: Good. So how about agreeing to the three-times-a-day practice again for the whole week?

Steve: Agreed.

Windy: And don't forget to look out for and challenge ideas concerning the terrors of tedium.

Steve: OK.

It should be noted that Steve did give a clue that his attitude towards tedium might be an obstacle to the completion of his homework assignment (see p. 63). I asked Steve whether or not postponing pleasurable activities would help him to overcome his predicted procrastination concerning the homework assignment. He stated that it would and I let it go. However, in retrospect I could have explored this a little further to determine whether or not Steve had an attitude of low frustration tolerance about the assignment. If I had done this I could have helped him to challenge this attitude and this may have encouraged him to tolerate the tedium better.

Step 13: Facilitate the Working-through Process

For your client to achieve enduring therapeutic change he needs to challenge and change his irrational beliefs repeatedly and forcibly in relevant contexts at A. In doing so, your client will further strengthen his conviction in his rational beliefs and continue to weaken conviction in his irrational beliefs. This is known as the working-through process, the purpose of which is for your client to integrate his rational beliefs into his emotional and behavioural repertoire.

Suggest Different Homework Assignments to Change the
Same Irrational Belief
When your client has achieved some success at disputing his irrational beliefs in relevant situations at A, suggest that he use

different homework assignments to change the same belief. This serves both to teach your client that he can use a variety of methods to dispute his target irrational belief (as well as other irrational beliefs) and to sustain his interest in the change process.

Discuss the Non-linear Model of Change

Explain that change is non-linear and that your client will probably experience some difficulties in sustaining his success at disputing his irrational beliefs in a wide variety of contexts. Identify possible setbacks and help your client to develop ways of handling these setbacks. In particular help your client to identify and challenge the irrational beliefs that might underpin these relapses.

In addition explain that change can be evaluated on three major dimensions:

1 *frequency* (does your client make himself disturbed less frequently than he did before?);
2 *intensity* (when your client makes himself disturbed, does he do so with less intensity than before?); and
3 *duration* (when your client makes himself disturbed, does he do so for shorter periods of time than before?).

Encourage your client to keep records of his disturbed emotions at point C using these three criteria of change.

At this point of the change process encourage your client to read Albert Ellis's (1984b) pamphlet, *How to Enhance and Maintain Your RET Therapy Gains*. This contains many useful suggestions which your client can implement to facilitate his own working-through process. It is reprinted in Appendix 2.

Encourage your Client to Become his own Counsellor

At this stage you can encourage your client to develop his own homework assignments to change his target irrational belief and to experiment changing his beliefs in different situations. Thus, if your client has been successful at disputing his irrational belief about approval in situations where he faces criticism at work, encourage him to dispute this belief in other situations in which he may encounter criticism — for example, with strangers or in social situations with friends. The more your client develops and carries out his own homework assignments, the more he will begin to serve as his own counsellor. This is important since as a rational-emotive counsellor, your long-term goal is to encourage your client to internalise the RET model of change and to serve as his own counsellor in the future after counselling has been completed.

Step 13: Steve

As noted in the previous step, Steve experienced some initial difficulty in disputing his irrational beliefs regularly. However, he made steady progress on this as the weeks followed and increasingly felt that he would be able to accept himself *for the possibility of failing* should he fail his PhD. This helped him to overcome his procrastination, although this problem also involved attitudes of low frustration tolerance and rebellion that were also tackled (see Part 3).

Later on in counselling Steve 'worked through' his fear of failure by resuming writing poetry, an activity he had given up years earlier due to his anxiety concerning the quality of his work ('I must write good poetry and would be a failure if I didn't'). He submitted several poems for publication, all of which were rejected, a situation to which he responded with disappointment rather than self-blaming depression.

Steve also gave two talks on his PhD thesis, something he had avoided doing due to anxiety concerning being criticised. ('I must give a good talk and would be a failure if I didn't.') He claimed that he was not anxious about these talks and accepted himself when several of his postgraduate student colleagues said that his talks were 'OK' or 'average'.

It should be noted that Steve achieved these gains with some difficulty. Thus, for several weeks he put off both submitting his poems and arranging to give his talks. It emerged that, like quite a few clients, Steve had the belief that it was easier to avoid his difficulties than it was to confront them. I brought this theme to the fore several times and helped Steve to see that while it might be easier in the short term to avoid his problems, it was harder for him to do so in the longer term. As will be shown in Part 3, when Steve fully confronted and challenged this avoidance-creating irrational belief, he made more consistent progress on his fear of failure and other problems.

In this part of the book I have reviewed the rational-emotive counselling *sequence* which outlines recommended treatment steps when your client has a *given* problem. However, clients rarely have only one problem and in Part 3 I outline the rational-emotive counselling *process* which discusses treatment issues that emerge during the beginning, middle, and ending of rational-emotive counselling and when your client has more than one problem.

Notes

1 When I refer in this book to the rational-emotive counselling *sequence*, I mean the steps you need to take to help a client with a *given problem*. In the next part of

the book I will discuss the rational-emotive counselling *process*. By this I mean the entire counselling process from beginning to end.

2 The gender of your client in this book was determined to be male by the toss of a coin.

3 As noted in Part 1 I refer to A as standing for activating events that may be regarded as consensual reality (that is, your client's descriptions about A can be confirmed as accurate by neutral observers) as well as your client's inferences about events. Note, however, that other RET counsellors prefer to group all cognitive activity under B while reserving A for the actual activating event, here referred to as consensual reality.

4 His feelings of other-pity may still be a problem for the client and this may be dealt with later in counselling. The point here is that it is not the most relevant one in accounting for his anxiety.

5 Rational-emotive counsellors frequently suggest to their clients that they tape-record counselling sessions for later review. This review often aids client learning.

PART 3   THE RATIONAL-EMOTIVE COUNSELLING PROCESS

In this final part of the book I will outline the rational-emotive counselling process and consider how the counsellor's use of strategies and techniques differs at different stages of the process.

While it is impossible to differentiate clearly between different stages of the counselling process, for the sake of clarity I will consider the beginning, middle, and ending stages of counselling.

The Beginning Stage

Establish a Therapeutic Alliance

The first task for you as a rational-emotive counsellor is to greet your client and to begin to establish a productive therapeutic alliance with him. This will normally involve discussing his reasons for seeking counselling help, his expectations for counselling, and correcting any obvious misconceptions he has about the counselling process. You will also want to deal with such practicalities as fees, and frequency and length of sessions. However, your main task at the outset is to encourage your client to talk about his concerns, initially in an open-ended way while you communicate your understanding of his problems. It is important that you show your client that you understand his concerns, demonstrate an unconditional acceptance of him as a person, and establish your credibility as an effective counsellor. In rational-emotive counselling, establishing counsellor credibility is best done if you adopt a problem-solving approach to your client's concerns from the outset. In doing so you should preferably communicate to your client that you intend to help him as quickly as possible and that you take seriously the problems for which he is seeking help. This means, as has been shown in Part 2, that you quickly come to an agreed understanding with your client concerning which of his problems you are both going to address first. In order to establish credibility with your client it is also important for you to provide him with a clear rationale which makes the purpose of your intentions clear. You need to be flexible at this point since clients differ concerning the degree to which they benefit from a problem-focused approach to counselling. You are advised to accommodate to your client's expectations on this point. With some clients, for example, you may need to explore with them, in detail, their life situations, and also perhaps the historical determinants of their problems before adopting a problem-solving focus. With other clients, however, you may enhance the therapeutic alliance by becoming problem-focused from the beginning. Here, as elsewhere, I suggest that you show a high degree of flexibility in modifying your approach to take into account both the treatment expectations of your client and the preferred mode of practice in rational-emotive counselling (that is, an early focus on problem-solving).

I have shown in Part 2 that there are thirteen major steps that you need to follow in dealing with any one of your client's given problems. Here I want to stress that it is important to adjust your mode of therapeutic participation according to the client with whom you are working. In doing so you will strengthen the therapeutic alliance. Thus, you may need to vary the pace of your interventions with different clients. Some clients think very quickly and will therefore respond to a fairly rapid intervention approach. Others, however, process information much more slowly and with these clients you need to reduce the speed at which you talk and the pace of your interventions. Since rational-emotive counselling is first and foremost an educational approach to counselling, you should respect your client's pace and way of learning and adjust your therapeutic interventions accordingly. If you work quite slowly with a client who would respond better to a more rapid exchange, then that client may become frustrated and may conclude that you are not helping him quickly enough. However, another client may find that you talk too quickly and deal with concepts too rapidly and consequently may experience confusion at the outset. Realise that it is basically your responsibility to tailor your therapeutic delivery to the client you have before you. Do not expect that your client, when confused because he does not understand the points you are making, will readily disclose this to you. Thus, like all good counsellors, you need to be alert to your client's non-verbal cues to gauge his level of understanding.

Also bear in mind that at the beginning of the counselling process it is important to meet your client's preferences concerning your counselling style. Clients vary concerning the value that they place on different therapeutic styles. Some clients, for example, respond best to counsellors who are informal in therapeutic style, and who are self-disclosing and friendly. Other clients, however, will respond better to greater counsellor formality. Such clients are more concerned with the counsellor's expertise and value a more distant, 'professional' style.

My own approach to determining how best to meet clients'

preferences concerning my therapeutic style is based on a number of factors. First, I have found it valuable in an initial session to ask clients questions concerning their prior experiences of receiving formal counselling and of being helped more informally with their psychological problems. In doing so I focus the discussion on the factors that clients have found both helpful and unhelpful in such 'therapeutic encounters'. I also ask them directly which particular style they would like me to adopt with them. As Tracey (1984) has argued, it is important to meet clients' initial preferences for counsellor behaviour if one is to develop a productive therapeutic alliance with them. Other rational-emotive counsellors obtain similar information from standard forms that they may use at the outset of counselling. Some employ, for example, Lazarus's (1981) *Life History Questionnaire*, which contains the following questions:

1 In a few words what do you think therapy is all about?
2 How long do you think therapy should last?.
3 How do you think a therapist should interact with his or her clients?
4 What personal qualities do you think the ideal therapist should possess?

Despite the use of such questions, please realise that the issue of adjusting your therapeutic style according to the unique requirements of particular clients is very much a matter of trial and error.

Some counsellors are uneasy about changing their therapeutic style with different clients. However, bear in mind that in your daily life it is very likely that you vary your interactive style with different people. It is likely that you interact differently with your family, strangers that you might encounter, colleagues at work, and dignitaries that you may meet in a formal setting. So you are probably familiar with the concept of being flexible in interactive style. In the same way I encourage you to adopt a stance of therapeutic flexibility and vary your counselling style according to the *productive* desires of your client. I stress the word productive here since, of course, not all clients' preferences for counsellor behaviour are necessarily therapeutic. In rational-emotive counselling, for example, it is important to avoid doing all the therapeutic work for your clients, to avoid meeting your clients outside counselling sessions for social purposes, and to avoid letting your clients lay on a couch while encouraging them to free associate.

Teach the ABC's of RET

Another task that you have at the outset of counselling involves teaching your client the rational-emotive model of emotional disturbance. First, encourage your client to understand that his emotional problems are determined largely by his irrational beliefs rather than by the troublesome events in his life. Secondly, help your client to understand that in order to change his dysfunctional emotions he needs to challenge the beliefs that he holds now, in the present, rather than engaging him in an overly long exploration of the historical determinants of such beliefs. However, as noted earlier, some historical exploration can be helpful, if only to strengthen the therapeutic alliance between you and your client. Thirdly, encourage your client to see that if he wants to gain lasting benefit from counselling he needs to put into practice what he learns during counselling sessions. This involves working repeatedly at changing his irrational beliefs and acting according to his newly acquired rational beliefs. You will have to go over these three major RET insights repeatedly before your client internalises them to the extent that he acts on them in his everyday life.

At this early stage of counselling your client is unlikely to be knowledgeable about the ABC's of RET. You thus need to take a focused active-directive approach to helping your client to learn the rational-emotive model of emotional disturbance. Wherever possible, encourage your client to think for himself by engaging him in a Socratic dialogue. Using this type of exchange help him understand that his emotional problems are largely determined by his irrational beliefs. However, at times you will need to use a didactic style of teaching your client the ABC's of RET. Whenever you do this at length, check whether or not your client has understood the points you have made (a point which I emphasised in Part 2).

Given that rational-emotive counselling has an educational focus, it is important that your client is clear concerning what you are trying to teach him (either Socratically or didactically). As such, it is important to remain focused on one problem at a time. Switching from problem to problem when your client has several emotional problems can be quite confusing for him and may interfere with the major points you wish your client to learn.

By the end of the initial stage, your client should have learned that it is his irrational beliefs that largely determine his emotional and behavioural problems. He should have had initial experience of detecting the irrational beliefs that underpin his initial target problem. He should be able to discriminate his rational beliefs from his irrational beliefs, and should have had some initial experience at disputing these irrational beliefs, using the logical, empirical, and pragmatic arguments outlined in Part 2.

This learning should be reinforced by homework assignments. At this stage such homework assignments may involve your client reading specific chapters concerning the ABC's of RET in one of the available RET self-help books (for example, Dryden and Gordon, 1990; Ellis and Harper, 1975; Ellis and Becker, 1982; and Ellis, 1988). In addition, you may ask your client to fill in one of the available rational-emotive self-help forms (for example, Dryden, 1982; see Figure 3).

Deal with your Client's Doubts

Given that clients have a wide variety of preferences concerning what approaches to counselling may be helpful to them, you may find at this stage that some of your clients may express doubts concerning the usefulness of rational-emotive counselling to helping them overcome their problems. One approach to handling such doubts is to encourage your client to persist with an open mind in using rational-emotive methods of change for a given time period (for example, five sessions), at the end of which you will review his experiences in using the approach. If, at the end of this period, your client continues to be doubtful concerning the usefulness of rational-emotive counselling to his problems, discuss his views concerning what type of counselling approach he thinks may be may helpful to him. A judicious referral at this stage may be more helpful to your client than encouraging him to persist with an approach to counselling about which he has serious doubts.

The Middle Stage

By the middle stage of counselling, your client should have gained some experience at disputing the irrational beliefs which underpin his target problem. Your client should have become accustomed to the idea that homework assignments are an important component of the rational-emotive counselling process, and may have had some experience of changing his irrational beliefs to their rational alternatives. While it is desirable for you to keep on track with a given problem (namely, the target problem) and to help your client through steps 1–12 of the rational-emotive counselling sequence outlined in Part 2, this is not always possible.

When to Change Tack

When your client has several problems, one of his problems other than his target problem may become more pressing during the middle stage of counselling. While it may be desirable to persist with the initial target problem until your client has reached a reasonable level of coping on that problem, to ignore the client's desire to work on a different and, to him, more salient problem,

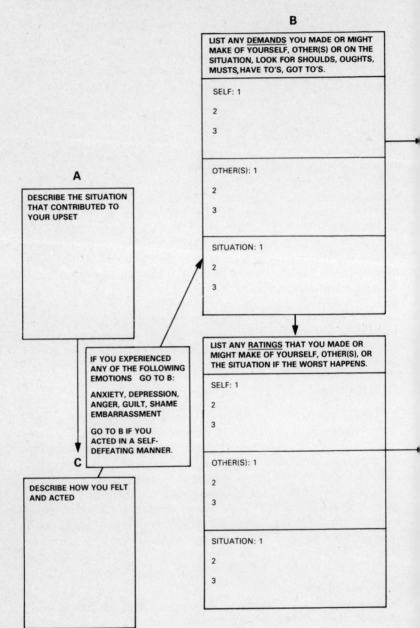

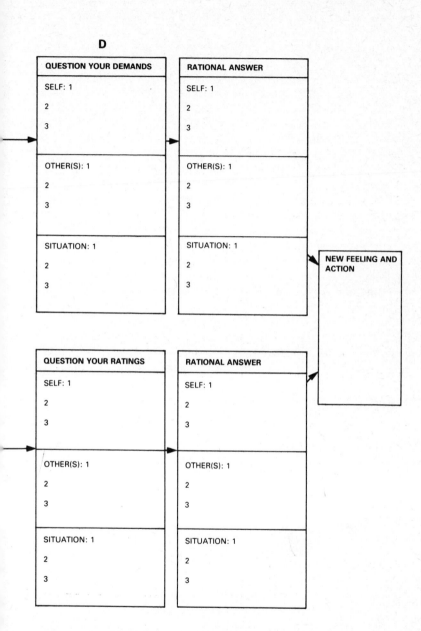

Figure 3   *A guide for solving your emotional and behavioural problems by re-examining your self-defeating thoughts and attitudes (Dryden, 1982)*

may unduly threaten the therapeutic alliance and you should avoid this if possible.

In my experience there are a number of good reasons to switch tack and to deal with a different client problem before he has attained coping criterion (the point at which the client is able to cope) on the target problem. The first indication that a productive shift in problem emphasis is indicated is when the client reports a crisis with the new problem. Imagine, for example, that your client's initial target problem is public-speaking anxiety. If he reports a crisis, namely that he has been physically abused by a family member and is experiencing emotional distress about this, then it is important to switch and to deal with this new problem. However, having made the switch, encourage your client to remain with the second problem until he has gone through steps 1–12 of the rational-emotive counselling sequence and has achieved coping criterion.

A second indication that it is important to switch to a second problem is when your client becomes emotionally disturbed in the session about this second problem and cannot concentrate on work on the target problem. If you try to continue to help him with his initial target problem you will rarely succeed and you will create the impression that you are more concerned with following your approach to counselling than you are with being empathic and responsive to the client's experience. Once again when you have switched to the second problem help your client to reach coping criterion on that problem by proceeding through steps 1–12 of the rational-emotive counselling sequence.

A final reason to switch to a different problem before you have helped your client to reach coping criterion on the initial target problem is when one of your client's other problems has become more pervasive than the target problem — that is, it pervades a greater number of areas of your client's life than does the target problem. Once you have switched to the new problem, again persist with it until your client has reached coping criterion.

If your client has several problems and wishes to deal with different ones before he has attained coping criterion on any one problem, give him a plausible rationale for remaining with one problem and for working on it until coping criterion has been reached. If your client still wishes to switch between different problems even after hearing your rationale, then do so to preserve the therapeutic alliance. However, if you suspect that your client is switching between different problems in order to avoid dealing with any one problem, then put this forward as a hypothesis for further exploration with your client. Once again bear in mind that while you may prefer to help your client to reach coping criterion on any one given problem before tackling a second or subsequent problem, you may have to be flexible to avoid unduly threatening the therapeutic alliance which by now you have established with your client.

Identify Core Irrational Beliefs

Whether you deal with your client's problems one at a time, switching from one to the other when the client has reached coping criterion on any given problem, or whether you have to compromise this ideal way of working and switch from problem to problem in order to engage your client fully in counselling, it is important that you look for common themes among the irrational beliefs that underpin his problems. Thus, if your client has discussed public-speaking anxiety, procrastination, anxiety about approaching women, and fear of being criticised by his work superior, begin to form hypotheses concerning the presence of core irrational beliefs which may be common across these problems. Thus, in the example that I have given, it may be that your client's problems concern ego anxiety related to the need to be approved. If this is the case, then as you work on a number of these problems you may suggest to the client that there may be a similarity between these problems with respect to the underlying cognitive dynamics. However, guard against making the assumption that all of your client's problems can be explained with reference to one core irrational belief, since this is rare. More common is the clinical fact that your client may have two or three core irrational beliefs. These, rather than specific problems, should become the focus for therapeutic exploration during this middle stage of counselling.

Encourage your Client to Engage in Relevant Tasks

Your major goal during the middle stage of rational-emotive counselling is to encourage your client to strengthen his conviction in his rational beliefs. This involves both you and your client using a variety of cognitive, emotive, imagery, and behavioural techniques which are all designed to encourage him to internalise his new rational philosophy.

Before discussing these techniques, however, it is important to note that as a counsellor you need to help your client:

1 to understand what his tasks are in counselling and how the execution of these tasks will help him to achieve his therapeutic goals;
2 to identify and overcome his doubts about his ability to execute his tasks;

3   to understand what your tasks are in rational-emotive counsel-
    ling and to see how your tasks relate to his tasks and his
    therapeutic goals;
4   to undertake tasks that he can realistically be expected to carry
    out;
5   to use therapeutic tasks in the sessions before you can expect him
    to put these into practice outside sessions;
6   to use techniques which are potent enough to help him to
    achieve his therapeutic goals.

Since the main burden of responsibility for promoting client
change rests on your client carrying out homework assignments
between sessions, it is important that you prepare him adequately
to execute such assignments. Thus, you need to:

1   provide a persuasive rationale for the importance of executing
    homework assignments in rational-emotive counselling;
2   negotiate with your client appropriate homework assignments
    rather than unilaterally suggest what these assignments should
    be;
3   negotiate assignments which are relevant to your client achiev-
    ing his goals;
4   negotiate assignments which follow on naturally from what has
    been discussed in counselling sessions;
5   specify as fully as possible what these assignments will be when
    your client is going to do them, and where and how he is going
    to execute them;
6   elicit a firm commitment from your client that he will execute
    these homework assignments;
7   encourage your client, whenever possible, to rehearse the
    particular homework assignment in the session. Your client is
    more likely to execute homework assignments successfully
    when he can picture himself doing so in imagery;
8   identify and overcome potential obstacles that may prevent
    your client from putting into practice particular homework
    assignments;
9   negotiate homework assignments which are not too time con-
    suming for your client;
10 suggest assignments which are challenging at a particular time
    for your client but not overwhelming for him.

Since the successful execution of homework assignments is such
an important part of rational-emotive counselling, it is very important that you check what your client's experiences were in
executing these assignments:

— Ask your client to report what he learned or did not learn from carrying out the assignments.
— Reinforce his *success* at executing assignments and, where necessary, reinforce his *attempts* at executing these assignments.
— Identify and correct errors that your client made in carrying out his homework assignments.
— Identify, assess, and deal with your client's reasons for not attempting or not completing his homework assignments. In particular help him to dispute his resistance-creating irrational beliefs.
— Encourage him to re-do the assignment.

Major Counselling Techniques
In this section I will outline the major techniques that are used to help your client to internalise his newly acquired rational beliefs.

Cognitive Techniques   The following cognitive techniques are used to promote belief change:

1 *Tape-recorded disputing.* Here your client records a disputing sequence on audio tape, playing both the role of his irrational self and his rational self. The goal of this technique is for him to ensure that his rational self persuades his irrational self that his rational beliefs are more logical, more consistent with reality, and will give him better results than his irrational beliefs.
2 *Rational coping self-statements.* Here your client repeatedly reminds himself of his rational beliefs as stated in short coping self-statements. You may encourage your client to write such statements on 5 × 3 cards which he can carry around with him and use as cue cards to remind himself of the appropriate rational messages.
3 *Teaching RET to others.* Here your client practises his new rational philosophy by teaching RET to his friends. During this process he has an opportunity to defend his rational beliefs and to point out to others flaws in their logic.
4 *Semantic precision.* Here your client becomes aware of his use of language when this serves to perpetuate his irrational beliefs. In particular you can encourage your client to identify such statements as 'I can't do X' and to replace this with 'I haven't yet done X.'
5 *DIBS (Disputing Irrational Beliefs).* DIBS is a structured form of disputing that is particularly helpful in the middle stage of RET. Here your client asks himself six questions and provides

answers which are relevant to the irrational belief that he has targeted to challenge and change.

(a) What irrational belief do I want to dispute and surrender?
(b) Can I rationally support this belief?
(c) What evidence exists of the truth of this belief?
(d) What evidence exists of the falseness of this belief?
(e) What are the worst possible things that could actually happen to me if what I am demanding must not happen actually happens?
(f) What good things could happen or could I make happen if what I am demanding must not happen actually happens?

6   *Psycho-educational methods.* These involve your client reading the rational-emotive self-help literature more extensively than in the beginning stage of RET and listening to audio cassettes of RET lectures on various themes.

7   *Referenting.* Referenting involves your client listing both the negative and positive referents of a particular concept such as 'procrastination'. This method is used particularly to counteract clients' tendencies to focus on the positive aspects of a self-defeating behaviour and to neglect its negative aspects. The purpose here is to encourage your client to focus on the negative aspects of self-defeating behaviours so as to provide him with an additional motivation to overcome such behaviour.

8   Further use of *cognitive homework forms* is suggested in the middle stage of rational-emotive counselling. However, once your client has become skilled at completing such forms, he is encouraged to do active disputing of his irrational beliefs without using the forms. Your client may be encouraged to keep using such forms, particularly when he experiences difficulty disputing his irrational beliefs in his head and when he begins to work on new problems.

Imagery Techniques   The following imagery techniques are used to promote belief change;

1   *Rational-emotive imagery.* The main imagery technique that rational-emotive counsellors use is rational-emotive imagery (Maultsby and Ellis, 1974). Here your client is encouraged to gain practice at changing his inappropriate negative emotion to an appropriate negative emotion at C, while maintaining a vivid image of the negative event at A. In doing so what he is in fact learning is to change his self-defeating emotion by changing his underlying irrational belief at B.

2   *Coping imagery.* These techniques are helpful in encouraging

your client to picture himself carrying out a productive behaviour in real life before in fact he actually does so.

3 *Time projection.* Here, for example, your client may state that a particular event would be 'terrible' if it occurred. You can indirectly challenge this belief by temporarily going along with this evaluation while helping your client to picture what life might be like at increasing intervals in the future after the 'terrible' event has occurred. In this way you are indirectly encouraging your client to change his irrational belief when he comes to understand that he can experience happiness again after the 'terrible' event has occurred and that he can either continue to pursue his original goals or develop new ones.

Emotive-evocative Techniques   These techniques encourage your client to fully engage his emotions in the change process while still having as your major goal helping him to identify, challenge, and change his irrational beliefs.

1 *Humorous exaggeration methods.* These can be used to encourage your client to see the amusing aspects of his irrational beliefs. Let us suppose that your client is anxious that other people may learn something 'shameful' about him. You could take this to a humorous and absurd conclusion by showing him that not only will these people actually find out about his 'shameful' secret, but that everybody else in the country will and it will be headline news in the daily newspapers for months. It is important to bear in mind that this use of humour should be directed at your client's ideas rather than at the client himself. Humour should be used sparingly and not with clients who would not consider such behaviour to be a legitimate part of a counsellor's role. Here, as elsewhere, it is important to bear in mind the importance of maintaining a productive therapeutic alliance when considering the use of humour.

2 *Rational humorous songs.* The purpose of rational humorous songs is again to help your client to take himself seriously but not too seriously. Ellis (1987a) has written a number of rational humorous songs and encourages his clients to sing them at moments when they might otherwise make themselves unduly psychologically disturbed. An example of one follows:

> *Perfect Rationality*
> Some think the world must have a right direction
> And so do I! And so do I!
> Some think that with the slightest imperfection
> They can't get by — And so do I!

For I, I have to prove I'm superhuman
And better far than people are!
To show I have miraculous acumen —
And always rate among the Great!

Perfect, perfect rationality
Is, of course, the only thing for me!
How can I ever think of being
If I must live fallibly?
Rationality must be a perfect thing for me!

3   *Therapist self-disclosure.* Another way of encouraging your client to internalise a new rational philosophy is to disclose not only how you as a counsellor have experienced a similar problem in the past, but also how you overcame it. Thus, for example, as noted in Part 2, I sometimes tell my clients how I overcame my anxiety about having a stammer and therefore stammered less. First I disclose how I used to make myself anxious by telling myself: 'I must not stammer, I must not stammer, it would be terrible if I were to stammer.' I then disclose how I changed this belief by disputing it and replacing it by the idea 'While I don't want to stammer, it's not the end of the world if I do.' I also mention that I practised this philosophy while deliberately speaking up at public meetings at every opportunity. In this example I not only tell how I overcame a problem similar to my clients by disputing my irrational belief; I also show them how important it is to do so while acting according to the rational belief.

4   *Stories, mottos, parables, and aphorisms.* You can use such stories, for example, to reinforce a rational message and to show your client that there are other sources of rationality apart from more standard disputing methods. Thus, for example, I often tell the story of the Buddhist monk who, while travelling with his apprentice, meets by a river bank a young girl who wishes to cross to the other side. According to his religion, however, the monk is not supposed to talk to the woman, let alone touch her, and yet he carries her across the river and puts her down on the opposite bank. After walking several miles further, his apprentice cannot contain himself and asks the monk why he carried the woman when his religion forbids him to do so. The Buddhist monk replies that his apprentice is still carrying her (that is, in his mind). This story is particularly helpful with clients who believe that there are absolute laws which forbid you to do something under all conditions.

5   *The use of force and vigour in disputing.* Ellis (1979b) has argued that the use of force and vigour in the disputing process is

particularly helpful in encouraging clients to internalise rational philosophies. You can encourage your client to repeat rational self-statements very forcefully or to engage in a very forceful dialogue with himself, particularly on audio cassette where he can encourage his rational self to challenge very forcefully the arguments made by his irrational self.

6 *Rational role reversal.* Once your client has shown some skill at disputing his irrational beliefs, you can adopt a devil's-advocate position in the counselling session, and present irrational arguments to encourage him to defend, and thus strengthen his newly acquired rational philosophy. In doing so you can also help to identify vulnerable points in your client's thinking, particularly when he demonstrates faltering acceptance of the rationality of his new beliefs.

7 *Shame-attacking exercises.* These are particularly helpful for clients who are ashamed about exposing some weakness in public. In using such exercises, you encourage your client deliberately to act 'shamefully' in public so as to gain practice at accepting himself for his 'shameful' behaviour and to tolerate the ensuing discomfort. However, it is important to safeguard against your client acting illegally or harming himself or other people. Encouraging your client to break minor social rules is particularly helpful in this respect (for example, wearing bizarre clothes designed to attract public attention).

Behavioural Techniques Critics often claim that rational-emotive counsellng neglects the use of behavioural assignments. However, this has never been true although the name of the counselling approach (rational-emotive) can give the wrong impression that RET does not use behavioural methods. On the contrary, rational-emotive counsellors consider that unless clients put into practice what they learn in counselling sessions through action then they will find it difficult to internalise a new rational philosophy. So you can encourage your client to use activity homework assignments whenever possible (for example, to confront fears and to court discomfort) while at the same time encouraging him to dispute his irrational beliefs cognitively. This simultaneous use of cognitive and behavioural methods places RET firmly in the cognitive-behavioural tradition of counselling.

Other behavioural techniques that you can use include anti-procrastination exercises where you encourage your client to push himself to start tasks sooner rather than later while putting up with the discomfort of undertaking unpleasurable tasks. Also, like their behavioural colleagues, rational-emotive counsellors advocate the judicious use of rewards and penalties to encourage clients to undertake uncomfortable assignments in the pursuit of their long-range goals. As Ellis (1985b) has noted, the use of stiff penalties is found to be particularly useful with clients who prove to be particularly resistant on certain issues.

Whenever possible, you should encourage your client to confront his fears fully rather than gradually. This is because full exposure methods encourage clients to overcome their philosophy of low frustration tolerance (LFT) more than do gradual exposure methods. Indeed, Ellis (1983c) has argued that the latter may even reinforce your client's LFT in that they may encourage him to believe, 'I must avoid making myself quite uncomfortable at all costs.' However, compromises on this issue often have to be made. Thus, when my clients find *in vivo* desensitisation methods based on flooding principles *too* 'overwhelming' for them at a given time, I encourage them to carry out an assignment that is challenging for them rather than one that they can do very comfortably.

RET also advocates the use of skills training methods (for example, assertion training). However, these are best used together with cognitive restructuring methods rather than on their own. It is this conjoint use of cognitive and behavioural techniques that distinguishes rational-emotive counsellors from their behavioural colleagues.

Additional Issues You will frequently have no way of knowing in advance which assignments your client will find helpful, and therefore you should use a trial-and-error approach to find this out. Also discuss with your client your intention to discover which techniques work and do not work for him, otherwise he may become discouraged when he uses a technique that does not lead to progress.

Since your main goal during this stage is to encourage your client to internalise a new rational philosophy, you and your client need to determine reasons for therapeutic change. Ideally your client should be effecting change by disputing his irrational beliefs rather than by changing his inferences about life events or the events themselves or by changing his behaviour. If you discover that your client has demonstrated therapeutic change without changing his irrational beliefs, reinforce his efforts but point out to him the importance of changing his irrational beliefs. Remind him of the rational-emotive hypothesis that long-term change is best achieved by philosophic change.

Deal with Obstacles to Change

It is during the middle stage of rational-emotive counselling that clients show most resistance to change. Assuming that your client has understood that his irrational beliefs do determine his emotional and behavioural problems and that he has gained some initial success at disputing his irrational beliefs, it is likely that his resistance to change can be attributed to his philosophy of low frustration tolerance (LFT). Frequently clients do not follow through on their initial successful change because they believe that 'Change must not be difficult' or 'I should not have to work so hard in counselling.' It is very important for you to be alert to the possibility that your client may have a philosophy of LFT about change, and if so you need to help him to challenge and change the irrational beliefs implicit in such a philosophy. Otherwise these beliefs will interfere with your client's attempts to internalise a new rational philosophy.

Maultsby (1984) has argued that change itself can be an uncomfortable experience for clients. He refers to a state called 'cognitive-emotional dissonance' during which clients feel 'strange' as they work at strengthening their conviction in their rational beliefs. Encourage your client to accept that this feeling of 'strangeness' is a natural part of change and if necessary dispute any ideas that he must feel natural and comfortable all of the time. Grieger and Boyd (1980) have called this concern the 'I won't be me' syndrome.

You will encounter a minority of clients who internalise the theory of RET as a body of knowledge but who will not work towards putting this knowledge into practice. Such clients are often very knowledgeable about the theory and can quote extensively from various RET books, but often have an implicit philosophy of LFT which stops them from putting their knowledge into practice. They may also believe that their knowledge is sufficient for them to effect lasting emotional and behavioural changes. As with other clients, the ideas which stop them from putting their knowledge into practice need to be identified, challenged, and changed.

Encourage your Client to Maintain and Enhance his Gains
It is in the middle stage of counselling that your client will experience greatest variability in the progress he makes, sometimes going forward, sometimes backsliding. As a result you need to help him stay fully engaged in counselling by helping him (a) to deal with set-backs; (b) to maintain his progress and later, (c) to enhance his gains. Ellis (1984b) has written an excellent pamphlet on this issue which is reproduced in Appendix 2. I refer this to you for the variety of points made and suggest that you give a copy to your clients when the issues raised by Ellis become salient.

Encourage your Client to Become his own Counsellor
Another important task that you have as a rational-emotive counsellor in the middle-to-late stage of counselling is to encourage your

client to work towards becoming his own counsellor. I noted in the previous section on the beginning stage of rational-emotive counselling that you will often have to take an active-directive stance in helping your client to learn the ABC's of RET and to understand why his irrational belief is self-defeating and the rational alternative is more constructive. As you move into the middle stage of counselling, you will need to review such points. However, the more you do so, the more you should encourage your client to take the lead in the exploration, particularly in the middle-to-late stage of counselling.

When you first discuss a particular problem with your client, be active and directive, but the more you work on this problem, gradually reduce the level of your directiveness and encourage your client to practise self-counselling. As you work together with your client on a particular problem over the course of counselling, help him to internalise the rational-emotive problem-solving method. Encourage him to learn to identify troublesome emotions and behaviours, help him to relate these to particular activating events, and from there to identify his major core irrational beliefs. Then encourage him to dispute these beliefs for himself and to develop plausible rational alternatives to these beliefs. Your client's major task during this stage of counselling is to weaken his conviction in his irrational beliefs and strengthen his conviction in his rational beliefs.

Not only should you encourage your client to internalise the RET process of change, but you should also encourage him to look for links between his problems, particularly those that involve core irrational beliefs. Your goal should be to help your client to identify his core irrational beliefs across a number of settings and to dispute these beliefs. As noted above, while you should reduce the level of your directiveness as you help your client to deal with a particular problem, you may have to go back to becoming active and directive when the focus of therapeutic exploration shifts to a new problem. However, as a major goal of this stage is to encourage your client to begin to become his own counsellor, you should endeavour, even when working on a new problem, to encourage your client to take the lead in the exploration of this new problem.

During this stage of counselling you should increasingly use Socratic dialogue to encourage your client to do most of the work and you should keep didactic teaching to a minimum. In particular you should use short, probing, Socratic questions to check on your client's progress. Thus, when your client discusses his experiences in dealing with his problem between sessions you may ask questions such as the following:

'How did you feel?'

'What was going through your mind?'
'How did you dispute that?'
'How could you have disputed that?'
'Did you believe the new rational belief?'
'Why not?'
'What could you believe instead?'
'How would you know that this belief was true?'
'If you believe that how would you act?'
'Could you try that for next week?', and so on.

When your client responds successfully to your decreased level of directiveness over a period of weeks, then you may begin to start thinking about working towards termination (see next section).

The Ending Stage

The question of ending rational-emotive counselling arises when your client has made significant progress towards overcoming the problems for which he originally sought counselling and has shown evidence that he has been able to utilise the rational-emotive problem-solving method in approaching his problems. Discussion about termination may be raised by either you or your client. When you both decide that you will work towards termination of counselling this may be done either by decreasing the frequency of sessions over time or by setting a definite termination date. During this stage you can usefully encourage your client to anticipate future problems and to imagine how he would apply the skills which he has learned during the rational-emotive counselling process to these problems. Your goal should be to encourage your client to view himself as his own major source of solving problems and discussion should centre on how he can apply his problem-solving skills in a variety of settings.

Clients who have done well during rational-emotive counselling may well have ambivalent feelings towards ending the process. You may need, for example, to assess whether or not your client believes that he needs your ongoing help. This may be expressed by your client casting doubts on his ability to cope on his own or by him reporting a relapse before termination. The best way of dealing with your client's belief, 'I must have the ongoing support of my counsellor, because I cannot cope on my own' is as follows. First, encourage him to dispute this irrational belief in the usual way. Then urge him to conduct an experiment to see whether or not it is true that he cannot cope on his own. Help him to specify which aspects of his life he thinks he cannot cope with on his own and then encourage him to test this out as a homework assignment.

Whether you are working with your client towards a phased or definite ending, build in well-spaced-out follow-up sessions so that you and your client can monitor his future progress. In one respect there is no absolute end to the rational-emotive counselling process because in most cases you would probably want to encourage your clients to contact you for further help if they have struggled on their own for a reasonably long time to put into practice the rational-emotive problem-solving method without success.

When rational-emotive counselling has been successful and you are working towards termination with your client, bear in mind that what has been a significant relationship for your client and perhaps for you is coming towards an end. Thus, it is highly appropriate for both you and your client to feel sad about the dissolution of this relationship. I believe it is important for you to encourage your client to express this sadness and in doing so he may express feelings of gratitude for your help. While you may wish to encourage your client to attribute most of his progress to his own efforts (this is undoubtedly true since he had the major responsibility for carrying out homework assignments between sessions), if you believe you have done a good job then it is appropriate for you to say this to your client.

Sometimes your client may offer you a gift in recognition for the help that you have given him. My own practice is to accept a gift with gratitude as long as its value in monetary terms is not highly disproportionate to the occasion. Appropriate gifts in this regard are perhaps a bottle of alcohol, some flowers or a small figurine. Some clients, however, do have difficulty saying goodbye and difficulty in experiencing and expressing sadness about the end of a relationship. They may, for example, cancel their final session or try to introduce a light-hearted tone into the final session. While extending counselling at this stage for too long is not to be recommended, I do suggest that in such instances you first look for possible irrational beliefs that your client may have about saying goodbye and about experiencing and expressing sadness concerning losing an important relationship. Then, encourage him to use his skills to identify, challenge, and change the relevant irrational beliefs that underpin these difficulties.

The Rational-Emotive Counselling Process: Steve

In Part 2 I introduced Steve, a 26-year-old PhD student, who was referred to me by his friend for procrastinating on problems concerning his PhD thesis and difficulties in relating to his PhD supervisor. I outlined the rational-emotive counselling sequence when his target problem was procrastination. In this part of the book I wish to draw together my counselling work with Steve to show the rational-emotive counselling process in action.

The first time I saw Steve I asked him to tell me how he thought I could help him. He referred immediately to the fact that I had been helpful to one of his friends and said that his major difficulties revolved around his academic work and his relationship with his PhD supervisor. He had not had formal counselling before, but had sought help in the past from friends and a kindly uncle. In response to my enquiry about what was constructive about this help, he said that he had appreciated the way in which his friends and his uncle spoke 'man to man' with him. He considered it helpful that they did not patronise him and did not spend a lot of time sympathising with his feelings. He said that what was unconstructive about their help was the fact that quite often they would intrude too much by giving him examples from their own experience which distracted him from dealing with his own problems. I concluded from this that I would use counsellor self-disclosure sparingly, if at all. In response to my enquiry about what he meant by 'man to man' talk, Steve replied that it was a direct no-nonsense approach to dealing with his problems in a way which respected the fact that he was an intelligent, mature individual who wanted as quickly as possible to become self-sufficient. In response to my question concerning what for him would be the best way that I could help him, Steve said that he hoped that I would engage him in a dialogue and would point out to him aspects about his situation that he could not clearly see himself, but without telling him what to do and without unduly sympathising with him.

Steve further stated that from what his friend had told him, he thought that my approach to counselling would be helpful, and during this discussion he remarked that he certainly did not want to explore the historical determinants of his problems. He wanted to deal with his problems here and now and get over them as quickly as possible. It seemed to me that Steve was a very good candidate for rational-emotive counselling in that he would benefit from a reasonably active-directive approach to counselling and one which both encouraged him to put into practice as quickly as possible what he learned in sessions and was present-centred and future-oriented. I hypothesised that Steve would respond best if I adopted a therapeutic style which was businesslike and friendly without being either overly formal or overly informal. As stated above, I also noted that I would need to use counsellor self-disclosure sparingly, if at all.

After agreeing to meet weekly and negotiating a fee that was appropriate to the fact that Steve was a PhD student and was not in employment, we developed an initial problem list as shown in Part 2. We chose to work first on his procrastination problem and spent the first two sessions working quite productively on that problem (see Part 2). Steve made good progress on overcoming his procrastination initially, although it did become apparent that this problem was not only related to his fear of failure as discussed in Part 2, but also to a philosophy of low frustration tolerance (LFT) and an attitude of rebellion towards his supervisor. Steve's philosophy of LFT was expressed in the belief, 'I must only work when I feel like it.' He used the detecting, discriminating, and debating method of disputing his LFT irrational beliefs quite well and utilised a method of penalties so that unless he did two hours work a day on his PhD he would refrain from reading the newspaper, an activity which he immensely enjoyed.

However, Steve struggled, at least initially, concerning his anger-creating belief towards his supervisor, which was also a factor in his procrastination. Steve believed that since his supervisor was being paid a good salary to supervise him and to be helpful rather than to be obstructive towards him, he absolutely must do his job properly. Steve seemed to cling to this belief much more rigidly than he did to the beliefs that underpinned his fear of failure and LFT and eventually I had to show Steve very forcefully that unless he gave up this demand he would be defeating himself and would quite likely harm his future prospects. Initially Steve reluctantly ageeed to work on disputing his anger-creating demand and to replace it with a rational preference, 'I very much want my supervisor to do his job properly, but there's no reason why he absolutely has to do this.' I encouraged him to use forceful self-statements to experience keenly the difference between annoyance and anger on this point and helped him to see that if he gave up his anger, he was not condoning his supervisor's behaviour. This was because he had a preference, which was 'I really do not like my supervisor's behaviour.'

Using this line of argument I finally got through to Steve and we then considered how he might usefully confront his supervisor. This led to a discussion of Steve's anxiety in that he was scared that his supervisor might deliberately ruin his chances and either fail his PhD dissertation or sabotage his future prospects. Steve's prediction of his supervisor's retaliation was related to a prior irrational belief about being disapproved of. Here, Steve's irrational belief was 'I must not be disapproved of by my supervisor and it would be terrible if I were', a belief which led him to overestimate the chances that his supervisor would retaliate against him in the way that he feared. Once Steve had disputed that idea and replaced it with 'I would really not like my supervisor to disapprove of me and it would be uncomfortable but not terrible if he did so', he then realised that his inference about retaliation was coloured by his irrational beliefs (Dryden et al., 1989). However, I encouraged him to go with the worst scenario and to imagine that his supervisor had sabotaged him and prevented him from getting his PhD. This led once again to Steve's anger-creating belief which was expressed in a demand for justice and fairness. I again had a difficult time getting through to Steve on the point that while it would be highly desirable that justice exist in the world, there was no absolute guarantee that it had to. Once he had accepted this, again by using forceful rational self-statements and by carrying out forceful self-dialogues on audio tape, we discussed how Steve would handle the situation if his fears really did come true and his supervisor did actively block him from getting his PhD. Part of Steve's homework on this point was to consult the regulations of the University of London with respect to PhD thesis appeals, something which Steve in his anger and fury had not considered. Steve did so and considered that the procedures outlined in the regulations did provide adequate protection in instances where PhD supervisors did maliciously try to sabotage their students.

Steve and I then discussed how we might broach the issue of his dissatisfaction with his supervisor and we actively role-played this for two or three sessions with Steve helping me to take the role of his supervisor. Since there was evidence that Steve's PhD supervisor considered politeness to be a virtue in his students, I helped him to adopt a polite assertive stance in the role-plays until he considered that he could put this into practice with his supervisor. Steve then did so and surprised himself in feeling less anxious than he predicted. He was also surprised that his PhD supervisor gave him a sympathetic hearing.

While Steve had been maintaining his two-hour work schedule up to this point, even though he had found it a struggle, after this meeting with his supervisor he doubled his work rate and reported that he was experiencing a lot more enthusiasm for his work.

Up to this point in counselling we had focused on three major irrational beliefs:

1 I must not fail at important things and I'm a failure if I do.
2 Life conditions must be favourable to me and I can't stand it when they're not.
3 Other people must treat me fairly and justly and they are no good when they don't.

On further exploration it transpired that Steve had been avoiding situations that he predicted he might find pleasurable and enjoyable because of his ego-related and discomfort-related beliefs. I suggested to Steve that it might be helpful to look at ways in which he could overcome his fear of failure and LFT in other areas of his life in order that he could gain more experience of internalising a new rational philosophy in those areas. Steve agreed and selected two areas where he felt that both these irrational beliefs were holding him back from doing something that he wanted to do. As shown in Part 2 these related to his avoidance of writing poetry and of submitting his poems for possible publication, and his avoidance of giving public talks on his PhD topic. My prediction was, at this stage, that Steve would find it relatively easy to put into practice what he had learned concerning the RET problem-solving method and I hoped that he would quite quickly start writing poems and submitting them for publication and to arrange PhD talks. However, Steve experienced greater difficulty about doing these things than I had predicted. This difficulty was mainly to do with his belief that it was easier to avoid his difficulties than it was to confront them. My therapeutic stance at this point was to move from gentle to more forceful encouragement and I showed Steve that while it might be easier in the short term to avoid his problem, it was harder for him to do so in the longer term, and that the more he stewed in his own juice the more he would add to his own level of discomfort. Finally, Steve resumed writing poetry and did submit his poems for publication, and while he has yet to have any of his poems published, he reported that he is coping very well with having his work rejected. He has even written a poem about self-acceptance in the face of poem rejection! With respect to his PhD topic presentations, Steve reported that once he had given them, he was surprised that he took in his stride the statements of his fellow students that his talk was 'average' or 'OK' and once again he was able to accept himself for these less than rave reviews.

At this point Steve brought up the issue of terminating counselling and we agreed to meet once every six weeks for the following three sessions instead of the weekly sessions that I had been having with him up to this point. At the end of the third of these sessions Steve said that he would like to discontinue counselling although he did agree to come back in six months for a follow-up interview. At this last meeting Steve reported that he was getting on very well with his supervisor now and that they had even gone out for a meal. His supervisor was now giving him much more thorough feedback on his work. Steve was now working five hours a day with great enthusiasm and was looking forward to starting the write-up stage of his PhD thesis. He was still writing poetry and was now getting more pleasure out of the process than he had hitherto. He had also planned to give a talk on his PhD thesis at a a national PhD conference on economics.

At our last meeting (I have yet to conduct the six-months follow-up interview) I asked Steve what was helpful and unhelpful about the counselling process. Steve said that he had found it extremely helpful, particularly the fact that 'You refused to let me off the hook.' He likened me to a Canadian mounted policeman who doggedly followed the trail of his irrational beliefs and refused to be put off the scent. The only thing he claimed to find unhelpful about the counselling was the fact that he was seeing me in my study at home which contains a vast library of academic books, which at the beginning served as a further negative reminder that he was procrastinating on his own academic work.

Steve was fully confident at his ability to cope on his own, without my help, and as we had taped his counselling sessions he said that he would refer to these if he experienced any emotional difficulties that he could not initially handle himself. At the end of that final session Steve shook me firmly by the hand and looked forward to seeing me in six months' time. Altogether Steve and I had fourteen sessions spanning 29 weeks.

APPENDIX 1

Possible Reasons for not Completing Self-help Assignments

(To be Completed by Client)

The following is a list of reasons that various clients have given for not doing their self-help assignments during the course of counselling. Because the speed of improvement depends primarily on the amount of self-help assignments that you are willing to do, it is of great importance to pinpoint any reasons that you may have for not doing this work. It is important to look for these reasons at the time that you feel a reluctance to do your assignment or a desire to put off doing it. Hence, it is best to fill out this questionnaire at that time. If you have any difficulty filling out this form and returning it to the counsellor, it might be best to do it together during a counselling session. (Rate each statement by ringing 'T' (True) 'F' (False). 'T' indicates that you agree with it; 'F' means the statement does not apply at this time.)

1. It seems that nothing can help me so there is no point in trying.   T/F

2. It wasn't clear, I didn't understand what I had to do.   T/F

3. I thought that the particular method the counsellor had suggested would not be helpful. I didn't really see the value of it.   T/F

4. It seemed too hard.   T/F

5. I am willing to do self-help assignments, but I keep forgetting.   T/F

6. I did not have enough time. I was too busy.   T/F

7. If I do something the counsellor suggests I do it's not as good as if I come up with my own ideas.   T/F

8. I don't really believe I can do anything to help myself.   T/F

9   I have the impression the counsellor is trying to boss me around or control me.   T/F

10 I worry about the counsellor's disapproval. I believe that what I do just won't be good enough for him/her.   T/F

11 I felt too bad, sad, nervous, upset (underline the appropriate word(s)) to do it.   T/F

12 It would have upset me to do the homework.   T/F

13 It was too much to do.   T/F

14 It's too much like going back to school again.   T/F

15 It seemed to be mainly for the counsellor's benefit.   T/F

16 Self-help assignments have no place in counselling.   T/F

17 Because of the progress I've made these assignments are likely to be of no further benefit to me.   T/F

18 Because these assignments have not been helpful in the past, I couldn't see the point of doing this one.   T/F

19 I don't agree with this particular approach to counselling.   T/F

20 OTHER REASONS (please write them).

APPENDIX 2

How to Maintain and Enhance Your Rational-Emotive Therapy Gains

ALBERT ELLIS PhD
Institute for Rational-Emotive Therapy
New York City

If you work at using the principles and practices of rational-emotive therapy (RET), you will be able to change your self-defeating thoughts, feelings, and behaviors and to feel much better than when you started therapy. Good! But you will also, at times, fall back — and sometimes far back. No one is perfect and practically all people take one step backwards to every two or three steps forward. Why? Because that is the nature of humans: to improve, to stop improving at times, and sometimes to backslide. How can you (imperfectly!) slow down your tendency to fall back? How can you maintain and enhance your therapy goals? Here are some methods that we have tested at the Institute for Rational-Emotive Therapy in New York and that many of our clients have found quite effective.

How to Maintain your Improvement

1. When you improve and then fall back to old feelings of anxiety, depression, or self-downing, try to remind yourself and pinpoint exactly what thoughts, feelings, and behaviors you once changed to bring about your improvement. If you again feel depressed, think back to how you previously used RET to make yourself undepressed. For example, you may remember that:

(a) You stopped telling yourself that you were worthless and that you couldn't ever succeed in getting what you wanted.
(b) You did well in a job or in a love affair and proved to yourself that you did have some ability and that you were lovable.
(c) You forced yourself to go on interviews instead of avoiding them and thereby helped yourself overcome your anxiety about them.

Remind yourself of thoughts, feelings, and behaviors that you have changed and that you have helped yourself by changing.

2. Keep thinking, thinking and thinking rational beliefs (rBs) or coping statements, such as: 'It's great to succeed but I can fully accept myself as a person and enjoy life considerably even when I fail!' Don't merely parrot these statements but go over them carefully many times and think them through until you really begin to believe and feel that they are true.

3. Keep seeking for, discovering, and disputing and challenging your irrational beliefs (iBs) with which you are once again upsetting yourself. Take each important irrational belief — such as, 'I have to succeed in order to be a worthwhile person!' — and keep asking yourself: 'Why is this belief true?' 'Where is the evidence that my worth to myself, and my enjoyment of living, utterly depends on my succeeding at something?' 'In what way would I be totally acceptable as a human if I failed at an important task or test?'

Keep forcefully and persistently disputing your irrational beliefs whenever you see that you are letting them creep back again. And even when you don't actively hold them, realize that they may arise once more, bring them to your consciousness, and preventively — and vigorously! — dispute them.

4. Keep risking and doing things that you irrationally fear — such as riding in elevators, socializing, job hunting, or creative writing. Once you have partly overcome one of your irrational fears, keep acting against it on a regular basis. If you feel uncomfortable in forcing yourself to do things that you are unrealistically afraid of doing, don't allow yourself to avoid doing them — and thereby to preserve your discomfort forever! Often, make yourself as *un*comfortable as you can be, in order to eradicate your irrational fears and to become unanxious and comfortable later.

5. Try to clearly see that difference between appropriate negative feelings — such as those of sorrow, regret, and frustration, when you do not get some of the important things you want — and inappropriate negative feelings — such as those of depression, anxiety, self-hatred, and self-pity, when you are deprived of desirable goals and plagued with undesirable things. Whenever you feel *over*concerned (panicked) or *unduly* miserable (depressed) acknowledge that you are having a statistically normal but a psychologically unhealthy feeling and that you are bringing it on yourself with some dogmatic *should*, *ought*, or *must*. Realize that you are invariably capable of changing your inappropriate (or *mus*turbatory) feelings back into appropriate (or preferential) ones. Take your depressed feelings and work on them until you *only* feel sorry and regretful. Take your anxious feelings and work on them until you *only* feel concerned and vigilant. Use rational-emotive imagery to vividly imagine unpleasant activating events before they happen; let yourself feel inappropriately upset (anxious, depressed, enraged, or self-downing) as you imagine them; then work on your feelings to change them to appropriate emotions (concern, sorrow, annoyance, or regret) as you keep imagining some of the worst things happening. Don't give up until you actually do change your feelings.

6. Avoid self-defeating procrastination. Do unpleasant tasks fast — today! If you still procrastinate, reward yourself with certain things that you enjoy — for example, eating, vacationing, reading, and socializing — only *after* you have performed the tasks that you easily avoid. If this won't work, give yourself a severe penalty — such as talking to a boring person for two hours or burning a hundred dollar bill — every time that you procrastinate.

7. Show yourself that it is an absorbing *challenge* and something of an *adventure* to maintain your emotional health and to keep yourself reasonably happy no matter what kind of misfortunes assail you. Make the uprooting of your misery one of the most important things in your life — something you are utterly determined to steadily work at achieving. Fully acknowledge

that you almost always have some *choice* about how to think, feel, and behave; and throw yourself actively into making the choice for yourself.

8. Remember — and use — the three main insights of RET that were first outlined in *Reason and Emotion in Psychotherapy*, Ellis, 1962):

Insight No. 1: You largely *choose* to disturb yourself about the unpleasant events of your life, although you may be encouraged to do so by external happenings and by social learning. You mainly feel the way you think. When obnoxious and frustrating things happen to you at point A (activating events), you consciously or unconsciously *select* rational beliefs (rBs) that lead you to feel sad and regretful and you also *select* irrational beliefs (iBs) that lead you to feel anxious, depressed, and self-hating.

Insight No. 2: No matter how or when you acquired your irrational beliefs and your self-sabotaging habits, you now, in the present, *choose* to maintain them — and that is why you are *now* disturbed. Your past history and your present life conditions importantly *affect* you; but they don't *disturb* you. Your present *philosophy* is the main contributor to your *current* disturbance.

Insight No. 3: There is no magical way for you to change your personality and your strong tendencies to needlessly upset yourself. Basic personality change requires persistent *work and practice* — yes, *work and practice* — to enable you to alter your irrational beliefs, your inappropriate feelings, and your self-destructive behaviors.

9. Steadily — and unfrantically! — look for personal pleasures and enjoyments — such as reading, entertainment, sports, hobbies, art, science, and other vital absorbing interests. Take as your major life goal not only the achievement of emotional health but also that of real enjoyment. Try to become involved in a longterm purpose, goal, or interest in which you can remain truly absorbed. For a good, happy life will give you something to live *for*; will distract you from many serious woes; and will encourage you to preserve and to improve your mental health.

10. Try to keep in touch with several other people who know something about RET and who can help go over some of its aspects with you. Tell them about problems that you have difficulty coping with and let them know how you are using RET to overcome these problems. See if they agree with your solutions and can suggest additional and better kinds of RET disputing that you can use to work against your irrational beliefs.

11. Practice using RET with some of your friends, relatives and associates who are willing to let you try to help them with it. The more often you use it with others, and are able to see what their iBs are and to try to talk them out of these self-defeating ideas, the more you will be able to understand the main principles of RET and to use them with yourself. When you see other people act irrationally and in a disturbed manner, try to figure out — with or without talking to them about it — what their main irrational beliefs probably are and how these could be actively and vigorously disputed.

12.   When you are in rational-emotive individual or group therapy try to tape record many of your sessions and listen to these carefully when you are in between sessions, so that some of the RET ideas that you learned in therapy sink in. After therapy has ended, keep these tape recordings and play them back to yourself from time to time, to remind you how to deal with some of your old problems or new ones that may arise.

13.   Keep reading RET writings and listening to RET audio and audio-visual cassettes, particularly *Humanistic Pyschotherapy* (Ellis); *A Guide to Personal Happiness* (Ellis and Harper); *A New Guide to Rational Living* (Ellis and Becker); *Overcoming Procrastination* (Ellis and Knaus); *Overcoming Depression* (Hauck); and *A Rational Counseling Primer* (Young). Keep going back to the RET reading and audio-visual material from time to time, to keep reminding yourself of some of the main rational-emotive findings and philosophies.

How to Deal with Backsliding

1.   Accept your backsliding as normal — as something that happens to almost all people who at first improve emotionally and who then fall back. See it as part of your human fallibility. Don't feel ashamed when some of your old symptoms return; and don't think that you have to handle them entirely by yourself and that it is wrong or weak for you to seek some additional sessions of therapy and to talk to your friends about your renewed problems.

2.   When you backslide look at your self-defeating *behavior* as bad and unfortunate; but work very hard at refusing to put *yourself* down for engaging in this behavior. Use the highly important RET principle of refraining from rating *you*, your *self*, or your *being* but of measuring only your *acts*, *deeds*, and *traits*. You are always a *person who* acts well or badly — and never a *good person* nor a *bad person*. No matter how badly you fall back and bring on your old disturbances again, work at fully accepting yourself *with* this unfortunate or weak behavior — and then try, and keep trying, to change your behavior.

3.   Go back to the ABCs of RET and clearly see what you did to fall back to your old symptoms. At A (activating event), you usually experienced some failure or rejection once again. At rB (rational belief) you probably told yourself that you didn't *like* failing and didn't *want* to be rejected. If you only stayed with these rational beliefs, you would merely feel sorry, regretful, disappointed, or frustrated. But when you felt disturbed again, you probably then went on to some irrational beliefs (iBs), such as: 'I *must* not fail! It's *horrible* when I do!' 'I *have to* be accepted, and if I'm not that makes me an *unlovable worthless person!*' Then, after convincing yourself of these iBs, you felt, at C (emotional consequence) once again depressed and self-downing.

4.   When you find your irrational beliefs by which you are once again disturbing yourself, just as you originally used disputing (D) to challenge and surrender them, do so again — *immediately* and *persistently*. Thus, you can ask yourself, 'Why *must* I not fail? Is it really *horrible* if I do?' And you can answer: 'There is no reason why I *must* not fail, though I can think of several reasons why it would be highly undesirable. It's not *horrible* if I

do fail — only distinctly *inconvenient.*' You can also dispute your other irrational beliefs by asking yourself, 'Where is it written that I *have* to be accepted? How do I become an *unlovable, worthless person* if I am rejected?' And you can answer: 'I never *have to be* accepted, though I would very much *prefer* to be. If I am rejected, that makes me, alas, a *person who* is rejected this time by this individual under these conditions, but it hardly makes me an *unlovable, worthless person* who will always be rejected by anyone for whom I really care.'

5.   Keep looking for, finding, and actively and vigorously disputing your irrational beliefs which you have once again revived and that are now making you feel anxious or depressed once more. Keep doing this, over and over, until you build intellectual and emotional muscle (just as you would build physical muscle by learning how to exercise and then by *continuing* to exercise).

6.   Don't fool yourself into believing that if you merely change your language you will always change your thinking. If you neurotically tell yourself, 'I *must* succeed and be approved' and you sanely change this self-statement to, I *prefer* to succeed and be approved,' you may still really be convinced, 'But I really *have to* do well and *have got to be* loved.' Before you stop your disputing and before you are satisfied with your answers to it (which in RET we call E, or an effective philosophy), keep on doing it until you are *really* convinced of your rational answers and until your feelings of disturbance truly disappear. Then do the same thing many, many times — until your new E (effective philosophy) becomes hardened and habitual — which it almost always will if you keep working at arriving at it and re-instituting it.

7.   Convincing yourself lightly or 'intellectually' of your new effective philosophy or rational beliefs often won't help very much or persist very long. Do so very *strongly* and *vigorously*, and do so many times. Thus, you can *powerfully* convince yourself, until you really *feel* it: 'I do not *need* what I *want!* I never *have to* succeed, no matter how greatly I *wish to* do so!' 'I *can* stand being rejected by someone I care for. It won't *kill* me — and I *still* can lead a happy life!' '*No* human is damnable and worthless — including and especially *me!*'

How to Generalize from Working on One Emotional Problem to Working on other Problems

1.   Show yourself that your present emotional problem and the ways in which you bring it on are not unique and that virtually all emotional and behavioural difficulties are created by irrational beliefs (iBs). Whatever your iBs are, moreover, you can overcome them by strongly and persistently disputing and acting against these irrational beliefs.

2.   Recognize that you tend to have three major kinds of irrational beliefs that lead you to disturb yourself and that the emotional and behavioral problems that you want to relieve fall into one of these three categories:

(a)   'I *must* do well and *have to* be approved by people whom I find important.' This iB leads you to feel anxious, depressed, and self-

hating; and to avoid doing things at which you may fail and avoiding
relationships that may not turn out well.

(b)   'Other people *must* treat me fairly and nicely!' This iB contributes to
your feeling angry, furious, violent, and over-rebellious.

(c)   'The conditions under which I live *must* be comfortable and free from
major hassles!' This iB tends to create your feelings of low frustration
tolerance and self-pity; and sometimes those of anger and depression.

3.   Recognize that when you employ one of these three absolutistic *musts*
— or any of the innumerable variations on it that you can easily slide into
— you naturally and commonly derive from them other irrational conclusions, such as:

(a)   'Because I am not doing as well as I *must*, I am an incompetent
worthless individual!' (Self-damnation).

(b)   'Since I am not being approved by people whom I find important, as
I *have to be*, it's *awful* and *terrible!*' (Awfulizing).

(c)   'Because others are not treating me as fairly as nicely as they
absolutely should treat me, they are *utterly rotten people* and deserve
to be damned!' (Other-damnation).

(d)   'Since the conditions under which I live are not that comfortable and
since my life has several major hassles, as it *must* not have, I can't
stand it! My existence is a horror!' (Can't-stand-it-itis).

(e)   'Because I have failed and got rejected as I *absolutely ought not* have
done, I'll *always* fail and *never* get accepted as I *must* be! My life will
be hopeless and joyless forever!' (Overgeneralizing).

4.   Work at seeing that these irrational beliefs are part of your *general*
repertoire of thoughts and feelings and that you bring them to many
different kinds of situations that are against your desires. Realize that in
just about all cases where you feel seriously upset and act in a distinctly
self-defeating manner you are consciously or unconsciously sneaking in one
or more of these iBs. Consequently, if you get rid of them in one area and
are still emotionally disturbed about something else, you can always use
the same RET principles to discover your iBs in the new area and to
eliminate them there.

5.   Repeatedly show yourself that it is almost impossible to disturb
yourself and to remain disturbed in *any* way if you abandon your absolutistic,
dogmatic *shoulds, oughts,* and *musts* and consistently replace them with
flexible and unrigid (though still strong) *desires* and *preferences*.

6.   Continue to acknowledge that you can change your irrational beliefs
(iBs) by rigorously (not rigidly!) using the scientific method. With scientific
thinking, you can show yourself that your irrational beliefs are only theories
or hypotheses — not facts. You can logically and realistically dispute them
in many ways, such as these:

(a)   You can show yourself that your iBs are self-defeating — that they
interfere with your goals and your happiness. For if you firmly
convince yourself, 'I *must* succeed at important tasks and *have to* be
approved by all the significant people in my life,' you will of course
at times fail and be disapproved — and thereby inevitably make
yourself anxious and depressed instead of sorry and frustrated.

(b)   Your irrational beliefs do not conform to reality — and especially do not conform to the facts of human fallibility. If you always *had* to succeed, if the universe commanded that you *must* do so, you obviously *would* always succeed. And of course you often don't! If you invariably *had* to be approved by others, you could never be disapproved. But obviously you frequently are! The universe is clearly not arranged so that you will always get what you demand. So although your desires are often realistic, your godlike commands definitely are not!

(c)   Your irrational beliefs are illogical, inconsistent, or contradictory. No matter how much you *want* to succeed and to be approved, it never follows that therefore you *must* do well in these (or any other) respects. No matter how desirable justice or politeness is, it never *has to* exist.

Although the scientific method is not infallible or sacred, it efficiently helps you to discover which of your beliefs are irrational and self-defeating and how to use factual evidence and logical thinking to rid yourself of them. If you keep using scientific analysis, you will avoid dogma and set up your hypotheses about you, other people, and the world around you so that you always keep them open to change.

7.   Try to set up some main goals and purposes in life — goals that you would like very much to reach but that you never tell yourself that you absolutely must attain. Keep checking to see how you are coming along with these goals; at times revise them; see how you feel about achieving them; and keep yourself goal-oriented for the rest of your days.

8.   If you get bogged down and begin to lead a life that seems too miserable or dull, review the points made in this pamphlet and work at using them. Once again: if you fall back or fail to go forward at the pace you prefer, don't hesitate to return to therapy for some booster sessions.

References

Bard, J.A. (1980) *Rational-Emotive Therapy in Practice*. Champaign, IL: Research Press.

Beck, A.T. (1976) *Cognitive Therapy and the Emotional Disorders*. New York: International Universities Press.

Beutler, L.E. (1983) *Eclectic Psychotherapy: A Systematic Approach*. New York: Pergamon.

Crawford, T. and Ellis, A. (1989) 'A Dictionary of Rational-Emotive Feelings and Behaviors', *Journal of Rational-Emotive and Cognitive Behavior Therapy*, 7(1): 3–27.

Dryden, W. (1982) *A Guide for Solving your Emotional and Behavioural Problems by Re-examining your Self-defeating Thoughts and Attitudes*. London: Institute for RET (UK).

Dryden, W. (1984) 'Rational-Emotive Therapy', in W. Dryden (ed.), *Individual Therapy in Britain*. London: Harper and Row.

Dryden, W. (1986) 'Language and Meaning in RET', *Journal of Rational-Emotive Therapy*, 4: 131–42.

Dryden, W. (1987a) *Current Issues in Rational-Emotive Therapy*. London: Croom Helm.

Dryden, W. (1987b) 'Theoretically-consistent Eclecticism: Humanising a Computer "Addict" ', in J.C. Norcross (ed.), *Casebook of Eclectic Psychotherapy*. New York: Brunner/Mazel.

Dryden, W. (1987c) *Counselling Individuals: The Rational-Emotive Approach*. London: Taylor and Francis.

Dryden, W., Ferguson, J. and Hylton, B. (1989) 'Beliefs and Inferences — a Test of a Rational-Emotive Hypothesis: 3. On Expectations about Enjoying a Party', *British Journal of Guidance and Counselling*, 17(1): 68–75.

Dryden, W. and Gordon, J. (1990) *How to be a Happier You: Solving your Emotional Problems by Rational Thinking*. London: Sheldon Press.

Ellis, A. (1962) *Reason and Emotion in Psychotherapy*. New York: Lyle Stuart.

Ellis, A. (1976) 'The Biological Basis of Human Irrationality', *Journal of Individual Psychology*, 32: 145–68.

Ellis, A. (1979a) 'The Practice of Rational-Emotive Therapy', in A. Ellis and J.M. Whiteley (eds), *Theoretical and Empirical Foundations of Rational-Emotive Therapy*. Monterey, CA: Brooks/Cole.

Ellis, A. (1979b) 'The Issue of Force and Energy in Behavioral Change', *Journal of Contemporary Psychotherapy*, 10(2): 83–97.

Ellis, A. (1980) 'Rational-Emotive Therapy and Cognitive Behavior Therapy: Similarities and Differences', *Cognitive Therapy and Research*, 4: 325–40.

Ellis, A. (1983a) 'Failures in Rational-Emotive Therapy', in E.B. Foa and P.M.G. Emmelkamp (eds), *Failures in Behavior Therapy*. New York: Wiley.

Ellis, A. (1983b) 'How to Deal with your Most Difficult Client: You', *Journal of Rational-Emotive Therapy*, 1(1): 3–8.

Ellis, A. (1983c) 'The Philosophic Implications and Dangers of some Popular Behavior Therapy Techniques', in M. Rosenbaum, C.M. Franks and Y. Jaffe (eds), *Perspectives in Behavior Therapy in the Eighties*. New York: Springer.

Ellis, A. (1984a) 'The essence of RET – 1984', *Journal of Rational-Emotive Therapy*, 2(1): 19–25.

Ellis, A. (1984b) *How to Maintain and Enhance your Rational-Emotive Therapy Gains*. New York: Institute for Rational-Emotive Therapy.

Ellis, A. (1985a) 'Expanding the ABC's of Rational-Emotive Therapy', in M.J. Mahoney and A. Freeman (eds), *Cognition and Psychotherapy*. New York: Plenum.

Ellis, A. (1985b) *Overcoming Resistance: Rational-Emotive Therapy with Difficult Clients*. New York: Springer.

Ellis, A. (1987a) 'The Use of Rational Humorous Songs in Psychotherapy', in W.F. Fry, Jr. and W.A. Salameh (eds), *Handbook of Humor in Psychotherapy: Advances in the Clinical Use of Humor*. Sarasota, FL: Professional Resource Exchange Inc.

Ellis, A. (1987b) 'The Evolution of Rational-Emotive Therapy (RET) and Cognitive Behavior Therapy (CBT)', in J.K. Zeig (ed.), *The Evolution of Psychotherapy*. New York: Brunner/Mazel.

Ellis, A. (1988) *How to Stubbornly Refuse to Make Yourself Miserable About Anything – Yes, Anything!* Secaucus, NJ: Lyle Stuart.

Ellis, A. and Becker, I. (1982) *A Guide to Personal Happiness*. No. Hollywood, CA: Wilshire.

Ellis, A. and Dryden, W. (1987) *The Practice of Rational-Emotive Therapy*. New York: Springer.

Ellis, A. and Harper, R.A. (1975) *A New Guide to Rational Living*. No. Hollywood, CA: Wilshire.

Gendlin, E.T. (1978) *Focusing*. New York: Everest House.

Grieger, R.M. and Boyd, J. (1980) *Rational-Emotive Therapy: A Skills-based Approach*. New York: Van Nostrand Reinhold.

Kelly, G.A. (1955) *The Psychology of Personal Constructs*. New York: Norton.

Lazarus, A.A. (1981) *The Practice of Multimodal Therapy*. New York: McGraw-Hill.

Maultsby, M.C., Jr. (1984) *Rational Behavior Therapy*. Englewood Cliffs, NJ: Prentice-Hall.

Maultsby, M.C., Jr. and Ellis, A. (1974) *Techniques for Using Rational-Emotive Imagery*. New York: Institute for Rational-Emotive Therapy.

Passons, W.R. (1975) *Gestalt Approaches in Counseling*. New York: Holt Rinehart and Winston.

Persons, J.B., Burns, D.D. and Perloff, J.M. (1988) 'Predictors of Dropout and Outcome in Cognitive Therapy for Depression in a Private Practice Setting', *Cognitive Therapy and Research*, 12: 557–75.

Rogers, C.R. (1957) 'The Necessary and Sufficient Conditions of Therapeutic Personality Change', *Journal of Consulting Psychology*, 21: 95–103.

Tracey, T.J. (1984) 'The Stages of Influence in Counseling and Psychotherapy', in F.J. Dorn (ed.), *The Social Influence Process in Counseling and Psychotherapy*. Springfield, IL: Charles C. Thomas.

Trexler, L.D. (1976) 'Frustration is a Fact, not a Feeling', *Rational Living*, 11(2): 19–22.

Walen, S.R., DiGiuseppe, R. and Wessler, R.L. (1980) *A Practitioner's Guide to Rational-Emotive Therapy*. New York: Oxford University Press.

Index

In the following index, 'Rational-Emotive Counselling' is abbreviated to 'REC'.